TRADEMARKS

TRADEMA®KS

*A guide to the
selection, administration,
and protection of trademarks
in modern business practice*

JOHN D. OATHOUT

CHARLES SCRIBNER'S SONS/NEW YORK

Copyright © 1981 by John D. Oathout

Library of Congress Cataloging in Publication Data

Oathout, John D.
  Trademarks.

  Bibliography: p.
  Includes index.
  1. Trade-marks—United States. I. Title.
KF3180.016   346.7304'88   347.306488   81-4492
ISBN 0-684-16844-8   AACR2

1 3 5 7 9 11 13 15 17 19 Y/C 20 18 16 14 12 10 8 6 4 2

Printed in the United States of America

Contents

Preface

During my tenure as trademarks administrator in the marketing department of a large international corporation, I often needed a comprehensive guide such as the one I have compiled here. Many of the trademark problems and questions that arose almost daily were relatively routine, while others posed unique problems or contained fairly technical legal aspects. I needed a single reference to the basics of trademark administration, so that I could handle routine and nonlegal matters without seeking the advice of our trademark attorneys—and at the same time recognize when I should seek them out.

Based on my experiences, I know that many others in the same situation also need guidance. Frequent trademark misuses in all forms of advertising and often in news stories testify further to a lack of knowledge about proper trademark use in many quarters. Even an attorney not trained specifically in trademark law, but responsible for his company's trademarks, expressed need for a "how to" and "how not to" trademark administrative guide as an adjunct to tracking through court decisions to decide what action to take.

The success or failure of a trademark is the responsibility not only of lawyers, but also of marketers, their advertising agencies, designers, and often of personnel in public affairs or public relations. This book is intended for all these people—those with little or no trademark training or knowledge but with a need to know.

Let it be clearly understood that I do not offer or intend this book as a substitute for legal counsel. I am not an attorney nor is this a legal treatise. Throughout, I urge you to seek qualified counsel when legal problems arise. The book might well carry the subtitle "What you should know about trademarks before calling an attorney."

Considerable trademark literature is available, most of it authored by members of the legal profession, devoted to trademark law, theory, or philosophy and to interpretations of hundreds of court decisions involving trademark matters. Short articles appear from time to time in trade journals or in the daily press. I herewith acknowledge my debt to many of these sources.

Source material in this book includes works and articles by such authorities as Sidney A. Diamond, member of the New York Bar and formerly Commissioner of Patents and Trademarks, United States Department of Commerce; Julius R. Lunsford, Jr., formerly trademark counsel for Coca-Cola, largely responsible for the status of "Coca-Cola" as one of the world's most valuable trademarks; J. Thomas McCarthy, Professor of Law at the University of San Francisco; Jerome Gilson, member of the Illinois Bar and member of the Bar of the Supreme Court of the United States; the late Walter J. Derenberg, considered the Dean of the trademark bar; and a host of others, including many excellent publications of The United States Trademark Association.

Throughout my work with trademarks, I had almost daily contact with trademark attorneys from whom I learned most of what I know about trademarks, and I express my sincere thanks to them. If they or their colleagues in trademark law find within this book misstatements or misinterpretations of legal fact, such errors are entirely mine.

I am indebted, too, to my marketing colleagues whose questions or problems have served as the basis for many parts of the text. Much of the manuscript was reviewed also by James M. Oathout, J.D.; his suggestions and encouragement have been most valuable. Designer/consultant/author Ben Rosen also provided valuable suggestions based on his authorship experiences and in his review and critique of the initial draft of Chapter 11.

Many, many trademarks and trade names are mentioned or illustrated as examples throughout the book. The selection has been largely random. The number of trademarks that might be used for illustrative purposes is so large that for the most part any one could serve as well as another.

TRADEMARKS

1
What This Is All About

Today's television viewers often see and hear actor Robert Young appearing on behalf of General Foods Corporation. Mr. Young meticulously refers to his sponsor's product as "Sanka brand decaffeinated coffee." Never does he or any of his co-actors mention only "Sanka." It is "Sanka brand decaffeinated coffee" and sometimes "Sanka brand."

On the surface, it might appear Mr. Young and his partners overdo things a bit by using four words rather than the one word "Sanka" to identify the sponsor's product. Not so. Their phrasing, rooted in good trademark practice, stems from the constant diligence a trademark owner must maintain to protect a highly valuable business asset—a trademark.

The General Foods commercial is saying in effect, "The decaffeinated coffee we offer is identified by our trademark 'Sanka.' " In terms of good trademark practice, the point is made, perhaps obliquely to the viewer, that "Sanka" is not a synonym for "decaffeinated coffee." Rather, it is the *trademark*, the *brand* that General Foods owns and uses to identify its particular decaffeinated coffee and to distinguish it from competing brands.

Good trademark practice—what is it and why is it important? Are we talking about "trademarks" or "brands" or both? Or is there any difference? What is "bad" trademark practice? How is a trademark established in the first place?

Good trademark practice is putting before the public, by means of a unique word or symbol, the identification of a particular product or service in a manner that benefits the product or service and the manufacturer or merchant who offers it. It is building equity and goodwill into the word or symbol. It is guiding the

1

metamorphosis of an unknown entity through the marketplace to become a major business asset. "Kodak" was but an arrangement of five letters worth nothing when first put to paper.

Good trademark practice does not, of course, guarantee business success. On the other hand, poor trademark practice can be damaging and seriously so. Someone has written that if a factory is destroyed, it can be rebuilt, but if a good name is destroyed, the business may be lost forever. If you want to be the owner of a "famous brand name," you must make it famous. The care and diligence given the management of the trademark—the "brand"— can be a major factor in establishing fame for the mark.

Trademarks are intellectual property. They are creations of the mind, just as are literary efforts, music, art, and inventions. A trademark is unique in that once ownership in it is established, it may remain the property of that owner forever, so long as the owner keeps using it and uses it properly. Trademark ownership in the United States is established simply by putting the mark into commercial use. Registration of the mark with the U.S. Patent and Trademark Office, while providing specific benefits, is not a prerequisite of ownership. Good trademark practice dictates trademark registration.

The primary role of a trademark is identification: it points to the source and quality of the particular product or service on which it appears, and separates it from similar products and services offered by others. Consumers look for specific trademarks either to select or to reject products or services that they like or dislike.

When a particularly well-established trademark is seen or heard, an image forms in the mind pinpointing a company, a product, or a service: Kodak, Xerox, Pepsi-Cola, Quaker Oats, Life Savers, Coca-Cola, Texaco, London Fog, Chevrolet, Nabisco, Budweiser, Exxon, Sears, Borden, IBM, United Airlines, Mercedes, Purina, and so on. The image associated with these trademarks isn't just happenstance. Companies responsible for them have spent millions through advertising and promotion to promulgate a favorable image.

A large measure of that image stems from the consistency with which trademark owners use their trademarks to identify *their* products or services *of particular quality and use.* A consumer is entitled to a product from a particular source and of a particular quality when buying an item bearing a specific trademark. If the trademark is misapplied through ignorance, carelessness, or indifference, so that it does not properly fulfill its functions, the consumer may be deceived. The image and the trademark can be damaged or destroyed. A trademark must be associated consistently with a product's source and its quality.

Equally important is the consistency or uniformity with which the trademark is displayed or used, not only by the owner but by others as well. Abiding by the rules for proper trademark use is all-important, and the trademark owner must set the example. The owner must be relentless in correcting misuses whatever the origin. The Xerox Corporation constantly reminds us through advertising not to commit such affronts and atrocities to its famous trademark as "Make me a xerox of this," "She's busy xeroxing your report," or "We made twenty xeroxes of the specification." No! Never! Speak instead of "Xerox copiers" or "reproductions made on the Xerox copier." ("Make me a Xerox copy of this." "She's busy copying your report on the Xerox copier." "We made twenty copies of the specification on the Xerox copier.") Always capitalize "Xerox" and use it as a proper adjective followed by a noun.

The origin of the use of a mark on goods to identify the maker is lost in antiquity. It is virtually impossible to chronicle trademark development. Almost every major archeological find provides some clue or hint that the use of such marks dates back almost to the first goods made for royalty or for sale or trade. Evidence indicates that the finest craftsmen of ancient days sometimes displayed their own unique mark on the wares they prepared for royal households, as it added to their personal prestige. One may speculate, too, that somewhere in the first days of commerce the basket weaver, the sandal maker, or the potter or silversmith hung a sample of his wares outside his tent or shop as a mark of his trade to attract buyers.

The mark of a profession, while not a trademark in the modern sense, dates back for centuries. In the opening lines of Shakespeare's *Julius Caesar* the tribunes Flavius and Marullus question a commoner:

> FLAVIUS: Is this a holiday? What! know you not, being mechanical you ought not walk upon a laboring day without the sign of your profession? Speak, what trade are thou?

COMMONER: Why, sir, a carpenter.

MARULLUS: Where is thy leather apron and thy rule?

Guilds and trade associations were established long before
Shakespeare's time, and one may assume he based the sign of the
first-century B.C. carpenter's trade on fact rather than fiction.

The craft of the silversmith has been regulated in England
since the end of the twelfth century. Consequently, most English
silver articles bear marks that make it possible to trace the year,
the place of assay, and also the maker's name. The practice of
marking silver dates back possibly to the years of the Norman con-
quest. The maker's mark was introduced on gold objects in the
middle of the fourteenth century. In the early days of the trade
guilds in England, the guild mark was placed on swords to differ-
entiate the genuine article from swords made outside the guild.
Bakers were required to mark loaves of bread so that poor quality
could be traced to the source.

Frank I. Schecter, in "The Rational Basis of Trademark Protection"—an article many regard as a classic in the field—discusses
the historical roots of the trademark.[1] In the 1500s, a proprietary
mark was placed on goods, at the option of the trader, for the
benefit of illiterate clerks, or for identifying and reclaiming merchandise in case of shipwreck. The mark simply identified the
owner of the goods and did not show the source of production.
Regulatory or compulsory marks were introduced to make it possible to trace defective work to its origin, and to aid in the discov-
ery and confiscation of "foreign" goods where a guild had a
monopoly.

Many trademarks were introduced in the United States with
imported goods, or "migrated" to this country with the craftsmen,
manufacturers, and merchants who left their homelands to establish business and commerce here. Undoubtedly, the majority of
marks were "native" to this country as new businesses and new
enterprises were developed. One cannot make passing reference
to trademark growth in the United States without mentioning the
brands burned on the hides of cattle as a defense against rustlers.
Western novels or cowboy movies that use the cattle brand as a
major part of their plot are legion. The cattle brand was not a mark
of origin and quality in the modern trademark sense, but rather a

Graphic marks from an earlier day. **a.** W. & J. Sloane, in use since 1843;
b. Prudential's first Rock of Gibraltar, 1896; **c.** Buster Brown and Tige,
1904; **d.** Pepsi-Cola, 1898; **e.** Waltham, circa 1915; **f.** Malt-Nutrine,
circa 1913.

proprietary mark of ownership. But the word *brand* has long been associated with the identification of cattle belonging to a particular ranch.

With the growing use of marks to identify goods of a particular source and a particular quality, imitation of the more successful marks and fraudulent use of marks also grew. Laws were enacted early on in Europe to protect the marks identifying goods made by particular guilds, and later in Europe and elsewhere to protect the first in the market with specific symbols or devices marking their trade or wares. In some early laws, false use of a mark was punishable as a capital offense.

The first trademark law in the United States was passed by Congress in 1870. It was declared unconstitutional and replaced by the act of 1881. In that period of U.S. history, many trademarks and trade names became famous and have survived to this day. Others have fallen by the wayside. Advertisements and packages of the 1880s and 1890s proclaim the virtues of RUBIFOAM, a "delightfully fragrant and healthful liquid substitute for tooth powder"; James Pyle's PEARLINE washing compound; Dr. J. MacDonald's ALKALASKA blood and stomach bitters; Cluett's CROWN collars and MONARCH shirts (from $1.25 to $2.00, none finer); CUTICURA remedies for skin and scalp; Durkee's GAUNTLET brand select spices and mustard; Colgate and Co.'s CASHMERE BOUQUET soap; ROYAL baking powder; ANTI-DYSPEPTINE (no opium, no mercury); A. G. Spalding's STAR toboggan; AUNT JEMIMA's pancake flour; ELASTIC starch; UNEEDA social tea biscuits; Button's RAVEN GLOSS shoe dressing; IVORY soap; CAPACON healing water; DUPLEX adjustable corset (one dollar); COLUMBIA yarn; a block letter T within which are the words THE GREAT AMERICAN TEA COMPANY; THE TRAVELERS of Hartford, Conn.; LUCIDOGRAPH cameras; and HINDERCORNS (for foot care) are but a few random samples. The trademark for Samson cords is said to be the oldest registered trademark still in use (registration # 11210 issued in 1884). The trademark is the word "Samson" appearing above a drawing of the giant holding open the mouth of a lion.

The most recent federal law governing today's trademark practice in the United States is the Lanham Act, passed in 1946, and formally identified as the "Trademark Act of 1946, As

Amended, Public Law 489, 79th Congress. Chapter 540, approved July 5, 1946; 60 Stat. 427." Throughout this text, this law is referred to frequently as the Lanham Act.

Virtually every country has a trademark law. The laws may differ in detail, but generally agree in principle. Their intent is to protect a business from unfair competition and the public from imitations by means of a sign—the trademark (or colloquially, the "brand")—that is unique to the particular business and placed on its goods, identifying the business as the origin of the goods. Trademark laws serve many interests. The manufacturer or merchant is served in that the laws protect the trademark that directs customers to his product. The consumer is served in that the trademark directs him, without deception or confusion, to the goods he wishes to buy. Trademarks and the laws governing them are in the general public interest as they provide a means by which producers can ensure the benefits of their particular efforts; without them, deception of consumers would probably be prevalent. Trademark laws provide another service by preventing removal from the language and from common use, as exclusive trademark property, common words of the language, letters of the alphabet, numbers, colors, geometric shapes—the common tools of communication. Thus the laws are in the interest also of competitors who wish to prevent a monopoly of symbols, signs, or expressions giving information about the goods.

Today, the trademark is the backbone of competitive merchandising. It is a part of the customer's right to know. As a piece of information about the product, it can be just as important as specifications of size, shape, use, and the like. Julius Lunsford stated the case for trademarks most succinctly: "The trademark of the twentieth century has matured into an indispensable servant of our fabulous production and distribution of goods, a direct response to a practical need; a utility in great demand."[2]

Customers place a great deal of confidence in familiar trademarks. This confidence comes from a mental mix of several factors: the maker's reputation for product quality and service; the customer's satisfaction or pride of ownership; product durability; fulfillment of a specific need; initial cost, cost of operation, and maintenance; and, sometimes, trade-in value. "Quality" may be the word that sums it up best. "Source" is important, but in to-day's marketing, source to many consumers becomes primarily a factor of quality.

The actual number of trademarks (or "brand names"), trade names, and service marks in use throughout the world today is impossible to determine. Some 400,000 trademarks registered in the United States are currently in use. Since registration began in the United States in 1870, more than a million trademarks have been filed in this country. Many, many trademarks are in use without the benefits provided by registration. Worldwide, the number of registered and unregistered trademarks in use can only be guessed as in the multimillions. Whatever the total, it suggests the highly competitive and highly intriguing nature of selecting, estab-lishing, protecting, and maintaining a good trademark.

The selection, care, and nurture of trademarks cannot be left to chance, but should be a well-defined responsibility within a company's administrative structure. Virtually every company rec-ognizes the importance of the legal aspects of trademarks and pro-vides some degree of legal administration for them. A thesis of this book is that too little knowledge of trademarks and too little re-sponsibility for properly selecting, using, and controlling them is relegated to the people who actually use them—primarily the product marketers.

Generally, major trademark responsibility resides with com-pany attorneys or outside counsel who, in the press of a broad spectrum of legal matters, attend to trademarks only as important needs arise, and limit such attention to legal aspects. This is not a criticism of the legal profession. It is an entreaty, rather, to bring to their aid a variety of nonlegal professional talent, available in practically every company, informed and organized for the proper administration of trademarks. The nonlegal tasks for trademark administration, as proposed here, are not necessarily arduous nor are they costly in terms of personnel and time. But they are vital to trademark success.

Evidence appears almost daily—in advertising, on product packages, and in news items—of trademarks poorly chosen or poorly managed. Assets worth millions of dollars can be at stake.*

---

*As but one example of trademark value, the *Wall Street Journal* of July 17, 1980, reported the sale by Carling O'Keefe Ltd. of its Black Label and Red Cap beer

To select a good trademark, to establish it, to maintain it, and to enhance its value requires care and diligence. It must be handled carefully and guided through the marketplace with the same care and diligence applied to the product itself. If something goes amiss with the product, quality control usually shows it and the situation can be corrected before much damage is done. If through carelessness or neglect something goes wrong with the trademark, it may be too late. It may be beyond recovery.

The basic job of trademark administration is to establish, protect, and maintain for company use trademarks that are unique, the distinctive property of the company, and free of conflicts. Through administration and control, the job is to build an image of goodwill, value, and service into a word or symbol, and to enhance those values through enduring, consistent, and proper use. This requires constant vigilance against trademark misuse and corrective action. It is the battle against infringers who try to come as close as possible to imitating a famous trademark for a free ride on its goodwill. These are responsibilities that should be shouldered by trademark administration, an administration including but extending beyond the company's legal department.

Carefully selected and well-managed trademarks are a part of the company's image and almost always an advantage to it. Sloppy or loose control may diffuse the image and confuse customers. A rather large retail chain, now defunct, offered household goods and clothing to middle- and lower-income markets. Its outlets and products were variously identified, using different displays and forms of its basic trademark, almost as if the company could not make up its mind as to just who or what it wanted to be. The trademark appeared to be either out of control or at least very poorly managed. This is not to say that tighter control of the trademark would have cured the company's ills, but certainly the inconsistent use did far more harm than good.

In supermarkets, consumers can only be confused (or benumbed) by a plethora of brand names incorporating such words as *natural, new, super, giant, genuine, real, light, old-fashioned,*

trademarks in South Africa. According to the report, second quarter results for the brewing firm will show, as a result of the sale, "an extraordinary gain of $10.5 million (Canadian)." Values attached to certain other trademarks are discussed in Chapter 3.

true, easy, and many other descriptive terms, words used so generally and so broadly that they have become virtually meaningless and valueless in product branding. Originality in trademarks is at a premium.

Trademark administration falls broadly into three categories—selection, legal protection, and control of use. This book is written primarily about trademark selection and control. It is intended for company management, marketers, their advertising agencies, designers, and public relations offices. Attorneys and paralegals who are not trademark specialists may find it a useful reference. Although legal aspects of trademark management are discussed where appropriate, such discussions are not to be construed as the final or authoritative word. Any company confronted with legal problems involving trademarks should retain qualified counsel, as mentioned frequently in the text. I hope that the text will inspire strong trademark administration where such administration is lacking.

The United States Trademark Association

In 1978, The United States Trademark Association celebrated its centennial anniversary. This nonprofit organization is the only association in the United States whose members are devoted to developing and preserving trademark rights, and to continuing protection for both buyers and sellers of goods through the trademark concept.

The aims and activities of The United States Trademark Association (USTA) are worthy of the support of every company, association, or organization owning even one trademark.

When the association was founded in New York City by twelve manufacturers over a century ago, its stated objective was "To protect the rights of owners of trademarks, to secure useful legislation and treaties and to give aid and encouragement to all efforts for the advancement and observance of trademark rights." Through its continuing pursuit of this objective, the association has become an internationally known and highly influential organization.

Today, USTA membership stands at well over 1,300 leading trademark owners, lawyers, and other firms and individuals, not only from the United States but from some sixty-five other countries as well. Through its committees, publications, and annual meeting, the association keeps its members advised of all trademark matters of interest, both legal and nonlegal. It provides a forum for discussion and exploration of trademark concepts and problems. It supplies information to businesses, educators, government officials, the press, and the public concerning the appreciation for and proper use of trademarks. A list of the committees (other than administrative) provides further insight into the work and scope of the USTA: Advisory Committee for Trademark Affairs, Annual Review Committee, Committee on Product Substitution, Dictionary Listings Committee, Education Committee, Information Committee, International Advisory Group, International Trademark Committee, Lawyers Advisory Committee, State Trademark Committee, and Trademark Film Committee.

The administrative functions of the association are handled by an executive director, assisted by a full-time staff. Offices of the association are at 6 East 45th Street, New York, New York 10017.

USTA Publications

The paragraph that follows, which appears in several USTA works, best describes the scope and purpose of its publications:

> Trends and developments in the field are reported to members in regular Bulletins and the bimonthly journal, *The Trademark Reporter®*, the only authoritative journal devoted exclusively to trademarks. Trademark information for members' management personnel is provided in the *The Executive Newsletter*. Available to the general public are a number of

books published by USTA on all aspects of the trademark field. Additional interpretive material on trademark management, protection, and legislation is also available. USTA maintains a comprehensive library and an extensive reference file as well.

The USTA also has a short (twenty-minute) motion picture in which puppets present basic trademark concepts in a most entertaining fashion.

2

Terms of the Trade

The words making up the lexicon for trademark management are often ill-defined and inconsistently used. This difficulty is largely historical; the words have been misused and variously interpreted for years by attorneys and judges in numerous court cases. Sidney Diamond, writing in the *American Bar Association Journal*, states, "Efforts to standardize trademark terminology have been unsuccessful. . . . few judges have much experience in the field, and opinions frequently perpetuate or even embellish errors found in earlier briefs."[1] Frequent misuses by otherwise knowledgeable persons outside the bar also have contributed to the muddle.

The definitions given in this chapter should serve trademark administrators adequately as daily working tools. They should be aware, however, that these terms often possess ramifications and interpretations other than those stated here (or new ones might be created in future court cases), and these finer points should be left to trademark attorneys for resolution.

A trademark manager should become thoroughly familiar with the basic terminology, both for use in discussions with trademark attorneys and for understanding when treading into legal matters outside his or her ken or area of responsibility. Moreover, trademark managers or administrators are often called upon to discuss important trademark matters with persons whose knowledge of the subject is limited to sales of "famous brand" merchandise, and they must be able both to recognize their conferees' limited knowledge of trademarks and to explain quickly and clearly the basic terminology.

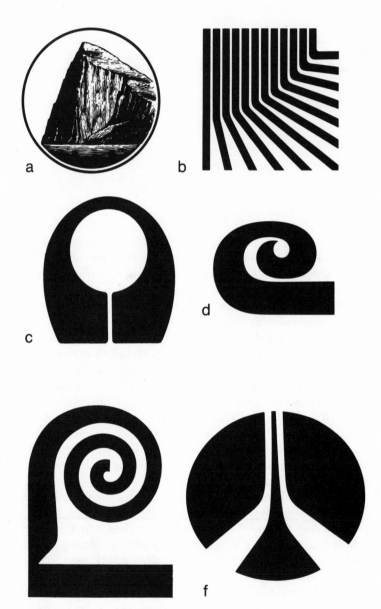

a

b

c

d

e

f

Examples of design trademarks: **a.** Prudential's present-day Rock of Gibraltar; **b.** Logistic Systems, Inc.; **c.** Acushnet Company; **d.** Celanese Corporation; **e.** Lawry's Foods, Inc.; **f.** North American Rockwell. Marks including both a design and words or letters, as in **g, h, i, j, k,** and **l,** are often referred to as "composite" marks.

Working Definitions

The "working" definitions presented here are believed to be the most common in current use. Historical variations and interpretations, while possibly of importance for legal considerations, have been omitted. These working definitions cannot cover all the ramifications of a particular term, and some questions of meaning may be left unanswered, but meanings will become clearer and most questions will be answered in subsequent chapters. For reference, the "official" definitions of many of the terms as they are stated in the Lanham Act are presented at the close of this chapter.

Trademark

A trademark is a word or symbol that a manufacturer or merchant places on his products to distinguish them from similar products offered by someone else.

Practically all trademark laws define "trademark" similarly and incorporate the same general concept—the trademark is a badge or sign placed upon a product to point to its source. For example, a model trademark law prepared for developing countries by the International Association for the Protection of Industrial Property defines a trademark as "any visible sign intended to distinguish the goods or services of one enterprise from those of another"[2] and Sidney Diamond defines a trademark as "a word or design used on an article of merchandise to identify it as the product of a particular manufacturer."[3]

Once established, a trademark becomes the sole property of its owner, so the trademark provides identification through which consumers select or reject merchandise of a specific origin. This does not mean, however, that the name and location of the maker or merchant must follow the trademark or necessarily be displayed in association with it. A simple analogy is the automobile license plate, which links the vehicle to its owner without stating the owner's name or address.

Among words established as well-known trademarks are Polaroid, Pepsi-Cola, Crayola, Band-Aid, Crest, Arrow, Esso, Kleenex,

TRADE · MARK

The likenesses of William and Andrew Smith (Trade and Mark) have been in use since shortly after the Civil War.

Timken, Volkswagen, Beefeater, Exxon, Cheerios, Mustang, Thermopane, Benrus, Zenith—to pick a few at random from hundreds of thousands.

Although registration of a trademark provides certain benefits to the owner, a trademark is established in the United States through use, not through registration, as explained in Chapter 6.

"Trademark" or "Trade Mark"? The predominant usage in the United States today is "trademark." Some package labels display the term as two words, among the more famous being the cough drop package showing the likenesses of the Smith Brothers, Trade and Mark. The Lanham Act may have been the impetus for changeover to a single word in the United States, as it always uses the term as one word. Outside the United States, the more common usage appears to be "Trade Mark" and sometimes "Trade-Mark." "Service mark" and "trade name" are written almost invariably as two words.

Brand; Brand Name

The words *brand* and *brand name* are not mentioned or defined in the federal trademark law. According to McCarthy, "The term 'brand name,' popular in business circles, has not developed into any legal term of art. It is merely a colloquial way to refer to a trademark."[4]

The United States Trademark Association *Glossary* defines *brand name* as "a word or combination of words used as a trademark."[5] This definition makes *brand* or *brand name* the same as *trademark* when limited to words.

Sales of "famous brand-name" goods ("we can't name the maker, but you will recognize it as soon as you see it") are legion. The use of "brand" rather than "trademark" is well understood by consumers. "What brand of coffee do you like?" invites a reply, while "What trademark of coffee do you like?" would elicit only a puzzled look. An advertisement's invitation to "compare our brand of pantyhose with other leading makes" suggests a trial of fit, appearances, snag resistance, and comfort, while "compare our trademark of pantyhose" would seem to offer an examination of the name rather than the goods.

Throughout this book, "brand" or "brand name" is used interchangeably with "trademark" when referring to word marks.

Examples of service marks in graphic form.

Service Mark

A service mark is the same as a trademark, except that it is used to distinguish a service rather than a product.

Merchandise may be offered in connection with the service, but if sales of merchandise are incidental and the service per se is dominant, a service mark is applicable. As with trademarks, service marks may be words or symbols or a combination of the two, and may apply to any of a vast array of services. Examples of registered service marks are Book-of-the-Month Club, Miss Universe, The Man from Nationwide Is on Your Side, CBS, NBC, Delta Air Lines, Baltimore Colts, Sesame Street, Chicago Symphony Orchestra, Weight Watchers, and The Champagne Music of Lawrence Welk.

Character names may be registered as service marks if the names are fictitious. Captain Kangaroo, The Supremes, and The Muppets are all registered as service marks.

A well-established, nationally recognized service mark.

As host to the 1980 U.S. Open, Baltusrol Golf Club registered this symbol for a wide variety of goods on which it was displayed and for the many services the club offered during the tournament.

A single mark may be used for both goods and services and protected for such use by registering it in the appropriate classes of goods and services.

Trade Name

A trade name identifies a company, whereas a trademark identifies merchandise.

Frequently the same word identifies both the company and its merchandise; whether it is a trade name or a trademark becomes a matter of the sense in which it is used. "Today, Xerox announced a quarterly dividend of . . ." is trade name use of Xerox, as it refers to the company. The appearance of the word "Xerox" on a copying machine manufactured by Xerox is trademark use, as it identifies the specific piece of equipment (for example, a Xerox 3400 copier) and points to its source.

Just as frequently, the trade name and the trademark are different words. Under the trade name Johnson & Johnson, that company manufacturers adhesive bandages bearing the trademark Band-Aid, among many other health care products.

Other examples of trade names include Amstar, Black & Decker, Conoco, Johns-Manville, Libbey-Owens-Ford, Hershey, Metropolitan Life, Nabisco, Upjohn, and so on. Stock exchange transactions are listed by trade names or their abbreviations.

Trade names may not be registered as such under the federal

trademark act in the United States. If the names are used also to identify products, they of course may be registered as trademarks. Common law rights to a trade name can be acquired and the name protected under common law when the name has been used consistently to identify a business. Trademark laws of several states provide for registration of trade names.

House Mark

"House mark" is defined in the USTA *Glossary* as "a primary mark of a business concern used on or in connection with a variety of products originating with it; usually used in association with another or secondary mark." The term is not defined or mentioned in the Lanham Act. When a trademark is used as a house mark, it is generally along the following lines.

A company offers a wide variety of products, each of which either bears its own identifying trademark or is identified solely by generic terms. The company chooses to display its name prominently—usually in unique or trademark form—on all its packages or labels to indicate it is the source of all its products, in addition to displaying the individual product trademarks or generics. In this sense, the trademark that identifies the company is a house mark, also sometimes referred to as an "umbrella" mark.

Sears, Roebuck and Company applies its Sears rectangular logotype to many of its branded products. It is displayed on Craftsman tools, Kenmore appliances, Die Hard batteries, The Steady Rider shock absorbers, Ted Williams sporting goods, and many other brand-name products, as well as on goods identified by generic terms only: paints, articles of clothing, hardware items, and others. Here, the Sears logotype trademark is the house mark, while Kenmore, Craftsman, Die Hard, The Steady Rider, and Ted Williams are trademarks of Sears for specific products.

The Borden trademark (see page 22) appears as a house mark on a wide variety of products that also display an individual product trademark.

Examples of the many Borden products carrying such dual identification are Cracker Jack candied popcorn and peanuts; Campfire marshmallows; several types of Elmer's adhesives; Kava instant coffee; Creamette pasta; Wall-Tex wall coverings; Wise

potato chips and other Wise snacks; Mirra-coat food supplement for dogs; Krylon spray paints, enamels and other spray coatings; Colonial cane sugar; ReaLemon lemon juice and ReaLemon lemonade mix; and a wide variety of other foods and household items.

Certification Mark

The certification mark may be considered the "stamp of approval" issued by an association to the individual businesses making up its membership and whose products or services conform to association standards. The association owning the certification mark neither manufactures nor sells the goods or services.

Examples of certification marks registered for goods include

Bonderized, Certified Indian River Fruit, Electric Living Award, and Du Pont Carpet Nylon. Among those registered for services are Adequate Wiring Certified, Life Master, Owner Manager National Hotel Association, and Your Independent Insurance Agent Serves You First. Many certification marks have accompanying designs.

Collective Mark

A collective mark indicates membership in an organization. Examples of registered collective marks include American Bar Association, Accredited Farm Manager, Classic Car Club of America, Lions International, National Hockey League, The Ohio State University, Realtor, Realtors, and Realtor–Associates, Phi Beta Kappa, National Dairy Council, and many others, some with designs.

Mark

"Mark" is a catchall term for all the various forms entitled to registration: trademarks, service marks, certification marks, and collective marks.

An example of a collective mark in graphic form.

Registration

Trademark registration consists of filing an application with a government and being issued a registration certificate. National registrations, issued in the United States by the United States Patent and Trademark Office, have no validity in foreign countries. Although U.S. registrations may serve as the basis for registration in some countries, registrations must be filed in each of the countries where protection is desired. Each state of the United States also provides for registrations.

Registration provides *prima facie* evidence of trademark ownership and provides other benefits as discussed in Chapter 6.

Registration Notice

Registered marks may be indicated in print and on packages by means of the symbol ®, or use of the statement "Registered in U.S. Patent and Trademark Office" or "Reg. U.S. Pat. & Tm. Off." Fraudulent use of a registration notice on marks that are not registered could result in loss of all rights to the marks.

The letters "TM" with a trademark or "SM" with a service mark may be used as a means of public notice of claim to trademark rights with marks that are not registered. Display of these letters does not, however, provide the benefits obtainable through registration. They frequently are displayed with new trademarks when they are first put into use and before they are registered.

Classes of Goods

Trademarks are registered within particular classes of goods. Systems of classification by product categories were established primarily for convenience in filing the hundreds of thousands of trademark registrations. The system used by most governments is the International System, which is the one now used in the United States. Several countries have their own unique systems.

A manager of trademarks should be generally familiar with the classes of goods and services for which trademarks and service marks can be registered, and the rights and limitations within the particular classes of interest. Further discussion and a list of the classes of the International System are included in Chapter 6.

Generics

A generic word or term is that which is commonly used to identify a group or class of items or services. A simple test of genericness is to decide what most people would call an object or service if all identifying marks were removed from it: shoe, pen, chair, tire, clock, radio, oil burner service, office cleaning service, and so on.[6] The word *generic* does not appear in the Lanham Act; the Lanham Act term used as a synonym for it is "common descriptive name."

All generic terms are available for common use and cannot be registered as trademarks for the goods for which they are generic. Consequently, a trademark owner should never use or encourage use of his mark in the generic sense (i.e., as a synonym or "common descriptive name" for the type of product or service); otherwise, the mark may become a part of the common language, and thus of no commercial value. Good trademark practice dictates display of the generic term with the mark—Parker pens, Goodyear tires, Panasonic radios, and so on.

Generic words or terms are placed on product packages to describe the contents. Words and phrases such as *motor oil, breakfast cereal, high gloss enamel, peanuts, soup, size AAA, 1.5 volts,* or *Type II–A* are essential pieces of product information. Such generics are not part of the product brand, nor are any other common words that may be used to further qualify the product, such as *heavy duty* with *motor oil, low calorie* with *breakfast cereal, exterior* with *paint, dry roasted* with *peanuts* or *condensed* with "soup."

Common dictionary words, letters, or numbers form a multitude of trademarks and are registerable if not used in the generic sense. Greyhound with transportation services, Arrow with shirts, Camel with cigarettes, GE in stylized form as a mark for General Electric, and 6–12 Plus insect repellent are examples of common words, letters, and numbers used as trademarks.

A generic word in a foreign language is treated in the United States the same as the English language generic—it cannot be registered as a trademark for the goods for which it is generic. For example, "Stylo" could not be registered as a trademark for a pen, since *stylo* is French for "pen."

Secondary Meaning

Common dictionary words that describe a product, its quality, or its use frequently are used as trademarks. Such words may achieve status as registerable trademarks when consumers learn to associate such descriptive terms with a specific product or service from a particular source and the words thus have taken on a "secondary meaning." Examples include Pocket Book paperback books, Holiday Inn motels, and World Book encyclopedias. Secondary meaning is discussed further in Chapter 4 in relation to "descriptive" marks.

Infringement

Trademark infringement is commercial use of a mark without consent of the owner, with intent to cause confusion or to cause a mistake or to deceive. Infringing use may be in the form of a reproduction, counterfeit, copy, or deceptive imitation. It may involve any or all of the various commercial displays of a trademark, such as advertising, package labels, signs, point of sale merchandise, and so on. Infringement would cause customer confusion as to the source and quality of products when two identical or similar marks appear on the same or closely related products of different manufacturers.

Infringement is a form of unfair competition. It is, in a sense, trespassing on another's property. The first user of the mark is protected even though he or she might not have registered the trademark.

If infringement is suspected or evident, the matter should be handled by attorneys, not by a nonattorney trademark manager.

Abandonment

A trademark is considered abandoned under U.S. law when it has not been used for two consecutive years, or use has been discontinued with no intention of resuming it again.

More important, however, the manner in which an owner treats or fails to treat a trademark can be considered abandonment. "Acts of commission" or "acts of omission" that cause a trademark to lose its significance as an indication of source could be the basis for finding a mark abandoned. An "act of commission" might be, for example, encouragement through advertising to use a trademark as a common household word. An "act of omission" might be failure to display a trademark distinctively from other words in an ad or text, or failure to act on misuses by others.

Copyrights and Patents

Copyrights, patents, and trademarks are sometimes confused. Trademarks identify products, copyrights protect artistic and literary expressions, and patents protect inventions.

A copyright is a statutory grant to an author or artist that protects literary, dramatic, musical, and artistic works against copying by others, and in some instances it also protects performing and recording rights. It protects the form of expression, rather than the subject matter. Copyrights are the responsibility of the Copyright Office in the Library of Congress. The Patent and Trademark Office has nothing to do with copyrights.

A patent is a statutory grant to an inventor giving exclusive rights to the invention for a term of years (seventeen years in the United States). A patent is generally for an invention of a scientific or technical nature. Design inventions sometimes are patentable. Granted by the federal government, the patent excludes others from making, using, or selling the invention.

Some Common Misconceptions and Errors in Terminology

As mentioned at the outset of this chapter, trademark managers must be prepared to discuss trademark matters with people who have little knowledge of the subject and who treat the terminology as if one word is as good as another. Quite commonly, speakers or writers refer to "trademark" as the word or symbol that identifies a company and "brand" as the name of one of its products. While this may be a handy distinction for those particular speakers or writers, it perpetuates an error that adds to the confusion about terminology.

The term *trade name*—the name under which a company conducts its business—often is used incorrectly as a substitute for "trademark" or "brand," as for example in trade directory sections labeled "Trade Names" or "Trade Name Index," when in actuality the lists are of trademarks (brands) applied to products. In the past, "trade name" was used to distinguish words that became trademarks because they acquired secondary meaning. (Inherently distinctive marks were "trademarks" or "technical trademarks.") Today, "trade name" refers almost exclusively to a firm's commercial or business name.

Errors in using terminology can detract from the credibility of a speaker or writer. A highly placed government official, speaking in early 1978 before a large audience comprised mainly of trademark attorneys, made frequent reference to "generic trademarks," a contradiction in terms. A word cannot serve both as a trademark and as a generic term on the same label. "Generic trademarks" continues to be used by the uninformed or the unconcerned, particularly in reference to labeling prescription drugs.

A discussion of trademarks in a marketing textbook states that one method for protecting a mark is "to give actual notice to the public that the *brand* has been *copyrighted*" (italics added). A trademark (brand) cannot be protected under the Lanham Act through a copyright. It can be *registered*, which is something quite different from being copyrighted. A copyright notice, ©, next to a trademark is meaningless for protecting the mark under the Lanham Act.

These and other varied, imprecise, and sometimes colorful uses can only add to the terminology confusion and create trademark problems and misunderstandings.

Lanham Act Definitions

The following definitions, of which many of the above are paraphrases or interpretations, are quotations from the U.S. trademark law, "Trademark Act of 1946, As Amended," commonly referred to as "The Lanham Act."[7] Similar terms, when defined by the laws of other governments, may vary somewhat but basically incorporate the same concepts.

Trademark "The term 'trademark' includes any word, name, symbol, or device or any combination thereof adopted and used by a manufacturer or merchant to identify his goods and distinguish them from those manufactured or sold by others."

Trade name; commercial name "The terms 'trade name' and 'commercial name' include individual names and surnames, firm names and trade names used by manufacturers, industrialists, merchants, agriculturists, and others to identify their businesses, vocations, or occupations; the names or titles lawfully adopted and used by persons, firms, associations, corporations, companies, unions, and any manufacturing, industrial, commercial, agricultural, or other organizations engaged in trade or commerce and capable of suing or being sued in a court of law."

Service mark "The term 'service mark' means a mark used in the sale or advertising of services to identify the services of one person and distinguish them from the services of others. Titles, character names and other distinctive features of radio or television programs may be registered as service marks notwithstanding that they, or the programs, may advertise the goods of the sponsor."

Certification mark "The term 'certification mark' means a mark used upon or in connection with the products or services of one or more persons other than the owner of the mark to certify regional or other origin, material, mode of manufacture, quality, accuracy or other characteristics of such goods or services or that the work or labor on the goods or services was performed by members of a union or other organization."

Collective mark "The term 'collective mark' means a trademark or service mark used by members of a cooperative, an association or other collective group or organization and includes marks used to indicate membership in a union, an association or other organization."

Mark "The term 'mark' includes any trademark, service mark, collective mark, or certification mark entitled to registration under this Act whether registered or not."

Table 1: Trademark Terminology

Term	Definition or purpose	Examples
Abandonment	Nonuse of mark for two consecutive years. Also, some forms of improper use tending to destroy significance as indication of product source.	
Brand, brand name	Colloquialism for trademark.	
Certification mark	"Stamp of approval" for products or services issued by an association to its members.	Adequate Wiring Certified (services) Certified Indian River Fruit (products)
Classes of goods	Categories of products or services within which marks are registered.	
Collective mark	A mark for membership in a professional, trade, or service organization.	American Bar Association, Phi Beta Kappa, National Hockey League
Copyright	Protection of literary and artistic expressions. Unrelated to trademark registration.	
Generic	The common dictionary term by which an object or service is known.	Pen, ink, car, tape; first aid, dry cleaning, engine repairing
House mark	A unifying trademark applied to a variety of products each of which may display its own trademark or may be identified generically.	The Borden symbol applied to Elmer's adhesives, Mystik tape, and a variety of dairy and other products

Term	Definition	Examples
Infringement	Copying or imitating someone else's trademark and use, which confuses the public as to the origin or quality of the product on which it appears.	
Mark	Collective term for words, symbols, initials, or numbers or a combination that distinguishes similar offerings from different sources.	
Patent	Protection of functional and design inventions. Unrelated to trademark registration.	
Registration	Formal recognition by a government of trademark ownership.	
Registration notice	® or other symbol used with a *registered* trademark.	
Secondary meaning	Assocation of a common descriptive dictionary term with a particular product or service from a particular source.	Holiday Inn, World Book
Service mark	A mark applied to services.	Berlitz, Robo-Wash
Trademark	A mark applied to products.	Kleenex, Minolta, Lark, Bostitch
Trade name	The name under which a company carries out its business (i.e., its commercial name).	General Motors, Eastman Kodak, Firestone, 3–M, Exxon

3

Functions of Trademarks

A trademark is indeed the *mark* of a *trader*. In its public appearances, on product labels and in advertising, a trademark is a company's spokesman and silent salesman, conveying a variety of messages to consumers. If your trademark conveys the right messages, consumers seeing it will be encouraged to buy your product in preference to that of your competitors. If the messages are wrong, your product will be rejected in favor of another.

Once established, a trademark deserves protection, recognized by the courts, for the services it performs. Felix Frankfurter, as a justice of the United States Supreme Court, stated in 1942, "The protection of trademarks is the law's recognition of the psychological function of symbols. . . . Whatever the means employed, the aim is the same—to convey through the mark, in the minds of potential customers, the desirability of the commodity upon which it appears."[1] (See Appendix I for the quotation in full.)

If a trademark is to indicate a product's desirability to potential customers, it must perform four basic tasks: (1) identify the product, (2) indicate its source, (3) signify its quality, and (4) speak for its owner in advertising.

It is difficult to rank the importance of these functions, particularly in today's complex marketing structures. Historically, the trademark's function of indicating the product's source is probably the oldest, with the function of signifying quality not far behind. Both rank high in legal considerations.

These several functions of a trademark are so closely interrelated as to be indistinguishable in the minds of typical consumers who, for the most part, probably give the matter little thought.

They may recognize a brand as an old friend pointing to a familiar and reliable product, or as something unfamiliar perhaps worthy of further investigation at a more convenient time. A marketer, however, should be thoroughly familiar with the intent of his trademark. A lapse in any one of its functions may render the mark totally ineffective.

Product Identification

The first function of a trademark is to identify a product and distinguish it from similar products sold or made by others. In this way trademarks are essential to competition. They are a basic part of the foundation upon which manufacturers or merchants build the reputations of their products. The success or failure of an enterprise often can be related directly to the trademark.

Trademarks are the strongest possible deterrents to fraud and deception. Without trademarks to identify and distinguish products or services, consumers would have no basis for selection or rejection, nor any assurance a particular item is *the* product they are seeking. An alternative method of distinction, suggested by some who consider trademarks an unnecessary added expense, would be to label products generically with the pertinent facts of materials or ingredients, and an analysis of quality or performance under standard test conditions. Such labeling is in fact required today for certain types of products. Imagine, however, attempting to buy a shirt without such identifying labels as Arrow, Brooks Brothers, Hathaway, Van Heusen, Lacoste, or any of the many other brands, but rather having to study statements of textiles, fade resistance, tear strength, and probable shirt life to decide which shirt to buy.

Trademarks and what they stand for sustain competition, and they make shopping convenient, reliable, relatively easy, and reasonably fast.

Source Indication

It is a customer's right to expect all similar products bearing the same trademark to come from a single source. This does not mean that the trademark has to name or locate the product maker; rather, it indicates that a product bearing a particular label has the same origin, whatever its name or place, that the goods bearing that label have always had. The "source" may be the actual manufacturer, or it may be a distributor or seller of the goods who has applied his own brand. For instance, a wide variety of unbranded products may be purchased by a grocery chain for packaging and branding with the chain's own trademark (e.g., Ann Page products of the A & P chain). The "source" need not even be one physical location; some products are assemblies of parts made in different countries, while other products may be made in any of several plants across the country that all produce the same item. Trademark use can be licensed, but the trademark still functions as an indication of the product's source because the trademark owner is responsible for the manner in which various plants or licensees use his trademark.

Quality Indication

X A properly used trademark is a statement of quality. Customers seek a specific brand because they associate a particular level of quality with it. Wherever the product is purchased, the customer has the right to expect consistency of quality or performance. Wherever you refresh yourself with a Coca-Cola, you expect just that beverage and not some watered imitation using an inferior syrup. And the Coca-Cola people take great care to see that you do get a Coca-Cola when you order one. Equal care is exercised by their competitors at Pepsi-Cola.

A trademark is not a legal guarantee or warranty of quality. The brand connotes *consistency* of quality for similar products so branded, but not identical quality. For example, a product made from raw materials available in Maine may differ somewhat from the same product made with raw materials available in California because of raw material differences, and sometimes because of different manufacturing equipment or processes used on the materials. The overall quality of the Maine and California products is consistent, but not identical.

For certain types of products such as automobiles, television sets, typewriters, cameras, pocket computers, and so on, cus-

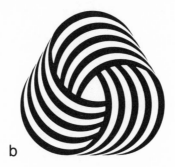

Symbols used especially to indicate quality: **a.** the mark of Cotton Incorporated, the organization representing America's cotton producers; **b.** the Woolmark, a registered certification mark of The Wool Bureau, Inc., the U.S. branch of the International Wool Secretariat.

tomers expect manufacturers to incorporate technical advances or improved materials and take such quality changes for granted. On the other hand, there are certain types of products for which an owner may risk loss of his trademark if he changes quality or ingredients without notifying the public. If the change results in a product that is inferior or wholly different from that for which goodwill was established, the product may no longer justify continued protection of the trademark.[2]

From the marketing point of view, the quality function of a

trademark cannot be overestimated and possibly may be its most important function. Today's buyers are much more highly informed about product quality by brand name than were buyers a few generations ago. Reports from consumer groups, professional testing organizations, radio and television consumer reporters, and government bureaus provide a vast array of quality data and product comparisons by brands. Pressures are mounting to establish and maintain product quality standards tied directly to health, safety, or economy. News items appear almost weekly about merchandise recalled by the manufacturer because of quality defects or newly discovered threats to health or safety.

Whether the product quality is fair, good, or superior, consumers soon associate that quality with the product trademark. They may select a product initially because of word-of-mouth or media advertising, but their satisfaction or dissatisfaction with it stems directly from personal experience with its quality or performance. The trademark becomes the signal for future purchase or rejection of the product.

Advertising

A trademark is a company spokesman in advertising, whether exposed in all available advertising media or solely by word of mouth. A trademark *is* a form of advertising. It serves to create knowledge of a particular product and a desire for it. Its use in advertising brings together all the other trademark functions—identification of the product, its source, and its quality. If the trademark has been used properly, the advertising function extends far beyond its appearance in the various commercial media. Customers pass along to friends and neighbors their reactions to particular branded products. Word-of-mouth can be the most powerful of all advertisements.

A Design Firm's View of Trademark Functions

A trademark performing the functions just discussed does not achieve status in today's markets through blind chance. A great amount of creativity, study, research, and testing go into a well-designed or well-chosen trademark.

In 1956, Lippincott and Margulies, Inc., an internationally known design firm, introduced the concept of "brandmark" to describe "the distinctive design used often as a part of a package or product. . . . A brandmark is often a trademark, a logotype, or the package itself."[3] Essentially, the L and M brochure described and assigned the term *brandmark* to what is commonly referred to as "trade dress"—a combination of distinctive features of a product, a label, or a package design that in addition to or along with the trademark contribute to the distinctiveness, fame, and success of a product. Certainly, within this concept, the trademark must be considered the key element that provides reassurance of product identification, source, and quality.

According to L and M, the "brandmark" must fulfill certain marketing-oriented functions. In most instances, these may be assigned to the trademark itself as the heart and soul of the "brandmark." (Indeed, within the L and M definition of brandmark, some forms of brandmark may be registerable trademarks.) Not every function must be served equally by every mark. The functions a brandmark must serve are listed as follows.

Institutional The mark must express certain characteristics that the company wishes to have associated with it: strength, quality, integrity, reliability, solidity, technical expertise, and the like.

Memory The mark must impress itself on consumers' memories to carry over from advertising to the point of sale, and from the initial sale to repeat sales. What counts is the recognition factor such as a girl under an umbrella with a container of salt under her arm, or the red-above-white label for cans of soup, or a large, M–shaped archway at a quick food outlet specializing in hamburgers.

Association The mark must provide consumers an immediate meaning in terms of a company or a product, for example, the top-hatted figure of Mr. Peanut; the bottle shape and lettering style of Coca-Cola; the circle surrounding a bell of A T & T.

Signal Stop! Do something! are signals or messages a mark should convey from retail displays. The mark should stand out from those of competition, enticing customers to look, pick up, examine, and buy.

Bridge   Particularly with packaged goods on supermarket shelves, the mark and its graphic display in an overall label design should convey all that is good about the product in actual use. Packages of laundry detergent may convey sparkle and cleanliness. The decoration of ice cream containers may suggest refreshing coolness, smoothness, and flavor.

Sales   In general, according to Lippincott and Margulies, a mark is more effective in its sales function when it expresses product qualities and personality than when it expresses company personality.

To the above six functions described by Lippincott and Margulies, another should be added for products marketed internationally: all connotations of the mark should be positive or at least neutral. Certain colors or color arrangements may have negative or undesirable significance in some countries. For example, purple signifies sorrow and suffering in the symbolism of some religions; red may signify bravery and courage, or it may connote danger. A perfectly good English word on a label may become derisive or obscene when translated into another language. Before exporting a product with its highly successful U.S. brand and label, make certain that the brand and package label convey the proper messages to consumers in the importing country.

Trademarks as Status Symbols

Another function of trademarks to many consumers is status symbol. To a degree, the use of certain trademarks as status symbols is related to the quality function, suggesting "I can afford the best (or the most expensive)." All automobiles serve the same personal transportation need, albeit some do it more reliably or more comfortably or more economically than others. Within the vast range of available makes and models, the Rolls-Royce ranks as one of the leading status symbols of today's worldly possessions. Remove the symbols that identify it around the world and the Rolls-Royce remains a superb vehicle—but without the glamor of its trademarks and the status they impart.

A trademark may become a status symbol because the merchandise it identifies has achieved the reputation of being the finest available. The manufacturer or merchant carefully builds an image of merchandise that is superior in materials, workmanship, and reliability, associated services that are impeccable, and usually price and exclusivity beyond the buying power of the majority. The trademark thus connotes a particular status of the buyers of such merchandise. Buyers who can afford and are interested in owning only the finest quality merchandise seek out the trademarks identifying such goods. Others buy the same merchandise not so much for its quality but because it aligns them in status with the first group.

The status of a trademark can be destroyed simply by lowering the quality of the product or its price or both. Years ago, the Packard ranked high as a status symbol among expensive American-built automobiles. The company added to its line a cheaper and less pretentious car, also under the Packard name and simulating the lines of the expensive model. Neither survived. Some have attributed the demise of the Packard directly to the destruction of its function as a status symbol.

Trademarks and Employee Morale

A trademark function that can be important to a company internally is its contribution to employee morale, pride, and sense of belonging. Witness, for example, the use of a company's trademark or trade name on uniforms, either for on-duty dress or for team sports. For many companies, a replica of its trademark cast in gold is its service award. Employees carry briefcases bearing the company mark, and sometimes wear neckties or scarves displaying it. The trademark becomes a symbol tying together a group of people serving a common purpose. Employees who wear or display the badge with pride can make a strong contribution to the company's image.

The Goodwill of a Trademark

Goodwill is that which is built into a business beyond its office building and factories, the products it makes, or the services it performs. It is the company's method of doing business, its concern for its customers, its attitudes, honesty, and integrity. Goodwill is all the positive but intangible things a company wants the public to think of it. In short, it is image and character, with a trademark as its symbol.

The goodwill of a business can be carried on its books as an intangible asset. The question of the goodwill value of a trademark arises in infringement cases, the sale of trademarks, the settlement of estates, and evaluation for taxes.

What is the goodwill of a trademark worth? Obviously, its determination is a matter for qualified accountants or attorneys or both. There are various formulas to evaluate a trademark's goodwill in terms of profits, years in business, and other factors. According to its former trademark attorney Julius R. Lunsford, Jr., in 1967 the Coca-Cola Company listed "Coca-Cola" and "Coke" at $3 billion as part of the company's intangible assets.[4] Lunsford cited other evaluations made some twenty years earlier: Maxwell House Coffee, $42 million; Jell-O, $35 million; Sun Maid Raisins, $5.6 million; Calumet Baking Powder, $32 million; and Castoria, $12.5 million. These evaluations are woefully out of date in terms of today's dollar and the current marketing status of the products, but they indicate the high value placed on the goodwill associated with the trademarks.

Characteristics and Types of Trademarks

The ideal trademark from a marketing viewpoint is simple, unique, distinctive, and memorable. It brings instant association with one particular product or service, its origin, and quality. It sells products or services and brings repeat sales.

To provide these benefits, a mark may be one or more words, letters, or numbers, a purely graphic symbol, or a combination of these. Which type serves best? The choice depends on many considerations, which boil down primarily to the purpose the mark is to fulfill. One type of mark may be perfect for a particular marketing situation but quite inadeqate for another.

A *word* mark is easily incorporated in texts such as advertising body copy, or in radio or other oral advertising and the discussions of sales meetings, product comparisons, and the like. It is found readily in telephone and trade directories. It needs no graphic standard for its reproduction (provided the use rules of Chapter 7 are followed). Certain types of word marks have inherent weaknesses, as discussed in later sections of this chapter.

On the other hand, a well-designed *graphic* mark may convey messages or meanings not conveyed by word marks alone—for example, strength, solidity, aggressiveness, modernity, conservatism, technical expertise, and so on. A symbol as a mark can often overcome language barriers. Also, on large signs along a highway it can provide distance recognition for the traveler or customer looking for a particular establishment, service, or product. Some people remember and recognize graphics more easily than words. A customer searching along the shelves of a supermarket or the racks of a clothing store often looks first for the symbol on the label or tag that identifies the origin of the product being sought. However, a well-designed graphic by today's standards may become outmoded in a decade as design concepts change. It then may be necessary to refurbish or replace the graphic to update it. Moreover, graphic marks do not lend themselves as readily to oral advertising or discussions as do word marks, nor to directory listings. To maintain the design purity of a graphic mark, reproduction artwork should be provided every time the mark is reproduced.

Words or symbols vary greatly in strength and ability to serve the trademark functions discussed in Chapter 3. The nature of a company or organization, its products or services, and its marketing objectives will dictate, in large measure, the functions of greatest importance and consequently the characteristics to be emphasized in creating the mark.

The appeal of a trademark, its acceptance in the market, and the degree to which it sells a product may be far more important than its legal strength. A legally strong, highly defensible trademark may in fact be dull and lack sales appeal. Of course, the ideal is a mark having both great sales appeal and legal strength. However, if a choice between the two must be made, sales appeal undoubtedly is the more important quality in most instances.

Word Trademarks

The strongest word trademarks, from the standpoint of legal protection, are coined or "fanciful" words having no dictionary counterpart. The weakest are those describing the product. Some that are weak legally may have strong sales appeal, but therein lies a problem. Because they are difficult to defend, they invite imitation and widespread use by many for a variety of goods. Such marks become highly dilute.

Table 2 lists types of words used as trademarks, with those having the greatest legal strength at the top.

A "fanciful" trademark is a word coined expressly to serve as a trademark. It is a combination of letters unlike any existing word. Dacron, Sanka, Exxon, Dreft, and Tylenol are examples.

Simply misspelling a common word does not make it fanciful. "Nu" for new, "tru" for true, "klam" for clam are not fanciful or

Table 2: Scale of Word Trademark Strength
(LEGAL PROTECTION)

Type	Examples	Secondary meaning necessary?
Fanciful (coined)	Kodak camera Yuban coffee Xerox copier	No
Arbitrary	Ivory soap Camel cigarettes Arrow shirts	No
Suggestive	Cyclone wire fence Chicken of the Sea tuna	No
Descriptive	Bufferin buffered aspirin Food Fair supermarkets	Yes

coined words when used in the sense of the proper spelling.

"Arbitrary" marks are common words in everyday use that, when used as a trademark, bear no relationship to the product. The word does not describe the product, nor indicate use or suggest a specific quality. The word *ivory* is distinct from any use or quality of the soap to which it is applied and certainly the soap contains no ivory. The GREYHOUND transportation system does not accommodate that particular breed of hound nor use it in its service. Shirts labeled ARROW have nothing to do with archery.

"Suggestive" marks often are difficult to distinguish from arbitrary marks. GREYHOUND, having nothing to do with the animals it suggests, is arbitrary, as mentioned. At the same time, it is suggestive of speed and trimness. HALO as a mark for shampoo suggests an attribute of the coiffure after use of the product. Or, since a halo as defined in the dictionary does not actually appear above the head of one who has shampooed, HALO could be considered an arbitrary mark. CYCLONE for wire fences is perhaps closer to suggestive than arbitrary, as it suggests strength under adverse conditions. COPPERTONE for suntan oil is a suggestive mark.

"Descriptive" marks are words that describe a particular use, size, class of user, ingredient, or characteristic of a product. To achieve status as a trademark that can be protected, secondary meaning must be established for the word; that is, the word must become associated with a particular product or service in addition to its primary meaning. According to Julius Lunsford, "A substantial percentage of trademarks in use today, including some of the most valuable and widely recognized, are marks which have acquired the cloak of secondary meaning."[1] Pocket Book is a trademark that describes particular paperback books. Holiday Inn describes a particular chain of motels. World Book describes an encyclopedia. Chap Stick describes a skin preparation in stick form. All these phrases have achieved secondary meaning, and status, as trademarks pointing to a specific source for the particular goods. To quote further from Lunsford:

> If plaintiff has used a certain word to refer to his product so long and so exclusively that in the minds of the consuming public that word or phrase has come to mean that "the" product is "his" product, and only "his" product, then such word or phrase has acquired a secondary meaning which equity will protect. . . . Extensive exclusive use and advertising over a long period of time is the most common method by which personal, geographical and descriptive marks are converted into distinctive badges of identification.

McCarthy devotes an entire chapter to "secondary meaning," citing many court cases and rulings involving interpretation of the term.[2] He lists, as types of words or symbols requiring establishment of secondary meaning to become registerable trademarks, words that are purely descriptive of the product, geographically descriptive words, personal names, corporate, business, and professional names, titles of single literary works, descriptive titles of literary series, noninherently distinctive signs and symbols, the overall appearance of trade dress and packaging, and noninherently distinctive product and container shapes. McCarthy points out that lists of examples based on prior court decisions are of little value in determining whether a given mark is descriptive. In addition to Pocket Book, Holiday Inn, World Book, and Chap Stick, already mentioned, his examples of descriptive marks for which secondary meaning has been achieved include Beer Nuts salted nuts, Bufferin buffered aspirin, Dyanshine shoe polish, Ivy League clothing, Rite-Fit furniture slipcovers, Tintz hair coloring formula, Sudsy ammonia, Savon gasoline, Navy Cut tobacco, Joy detergent, Joy perfume, Food Fair supermarkets, and many others.

McCarthy credits the Supreme Court of North Carolina for "an excellent capsule definition of secondary meaning":

> When a particular business has used words [publicly] for so long or so exclusively or when it has promoted its products to such an extent that the words do not register their literal meaning on the public mind but are instantly associated with one enterprise, such words have attained a secondary meaning. That is to say, a secondary meaning exists when in addition to their literal, or dictionary meaning, words connote to the public a product from a unique source.[3]

There are advantages and disadvantages to all four types of marks in the trademark scale of Table 2. Fanciful marks have the greatest legal strength and are easiest to protect against imitations. Creating a fanciful trademark can be hard work, time-consuming, and sometimes costly. To establish trademark significance for a totally unfamiliar word or design—a word or design the public will associate with a particular product and its source—may require large expenses for advertising.

At the other end of the scale, descriptive marks are quite weak legally and protection extends only to the particular products or services to which they are applied and only after secondary meaning is established. Some manufacturers might choose a descriptive trademark because they are satisfied to let the mark on the product package do the entire selling job. "High Strength" as the brand on a package of elastic bands might sell all of the product the manufacturer cares to make. He probably could not prevent others from offering HiStrength aspirin, or High Strength adhesive, or High-Strength children's hosiery. Or, a manufacturer may believe a highly descriptive mark will point directly to *his* product when a customer seeks a product having the particular use, quality, or other attribute that the trademark describes.

A mark that is too pointed in its suggestiveness or descriptiveness usually lacks versatility. If too closely associated with a specific quality use, the mark usually becomes obsolete when the product becomes obsolete. As a hypothetical example, "File-All" becomes well established as a mark for a card-filing system and equipment for handling various types of data. The system and equipment are made obsolete by computers. "File-All" as a trademark is no longer useful as it is too well known as a card system. To apply "File-All" to a computer system could carry with it an image of obsolescence. A more versatile and less descriptive mark might well be adaptable to changing technology and use with other products.

Initials and Numbers as Trademarks

Many companies have been quite successful in using initials or numbers or their combinations as trademarks. Because of long consistent use by the companies, we recognize GE, GM, RCA, A&P, ITT, AT&T, 3M, 3-in-One, 7-Up, V-8, Chanel No. 5, and many others. These are examples of particular combinations pointing to one source, that is, trademarks deserving protection.

An arbitrary arrangement of letters may serve as a protectable trademark, just as any other coined or fanciful word mark, without need to prove secondary meaning. However, letters that are an accepted abbreviation for a generic or descriptive term, such as "pvc" for polyvinyl chloride, are not recognized as trademarks.

Numbers alone or numbers combined with letters, because they may be descriptive, may need proof of secondary meaning to be registered and protected as trademarks. Numbers used only to indicate a model number, capacity, size, style, or grade are considered generic and cannot serve as trademarks.

As with generic words, letters of the alphabet and numbers

are common property. They cannot be cornered for exclusive use. Consequently it is extremely difficult to arrive at a unique combination that is not confusingly similar to combinations already in use. A recent Manhattan telephone directory lists, for example, thirty firms using A&S, twenty-two firms with E–Z, and about sixty with JJ or J&J. The first five columns of the directory are devoted to firms using the letter A singly and in multiples—up to nine A's!

"There is such a shortage of words available for trademarks that the use of the company's initials is a tempting alternative," writes Sidney Diamond, adding, "This route to trademark selection sometimes can be a source of trouble and frustration."[4]

One problem with initials and numbers, of possible consequence to marketers, is the way in which they are listed in telephone and trade directories. Bell System telephone directories list all combinations of initials at the front of each alphabetical section: AA, AB . . . AZ before Aaron; BA, BB . . . BZ before Baar, and so on. The Trademark Index in *Thomas Register of American Manufacturers* places initials in alphabetical order throughout each letter section (e.g., H, Haag, Hazelton, H&B, HB, . . . Hyzeen, HZ–L, etc.)[5]. The Bell directories list numbers alphabetically within each section as if written as a word. The 3M Company appears within the T's along with other companies using "Three" or "3." The *Thomas Register*'s Trademark Index lists all number trademarks at the end of the entire alphabetical listing, after all word and initial trademarks beginning with Z.

Some trade directories follow the Bell system, some the system used in the Trademark Index of the *Thomas Register*, and some appear to be a mixture of both, for initials and numbers. Telephone or trade directory listing can be important to a marketer. What may be considered an extremely clever use of initials or numbers as a trademark can result in directory obscurity, engendering frustration on the part of customers trying to find the company.

Personal Names as Trademarks

Any person should be able to use his own name to identify his own business. A personal name should not be set aside as the exclusive trademark property of one individual. However, through long and continued use on specific goods or services, some surnames have become sufficiently famous to achieve secondary meaning and are thus trademarks deserving protection: Smith Brothers, King C. Gillette, Levi Strauss, L. L. Bean, Black & Decker, Libbey-Owens-Ford, Brooks Brothers, H. J. Heinz, Stokely-Van Camp, Charles Scribner's Sons, and hundreds of others.

Just as with word trademarks, rights in a surname go to the first user when two identical or confusingly similar names are used as trademarks. Whether the second user is infringing upon the rights of the first appears to depend somewhat on the name's fame and whether the public, because of that fame, believes only one source is involved. Sidney Diamond cites, among other examples, Max Factor Hosiery of Beverly Hills, owned and operated by a real Max Factor, who was stopped from use of the name by Max Factor of cosmetic fame. The cosmetician had entered the business and had become famous long before the hosiery Max Factor. The two types of products, cosmetics and hosiery, are some-

what related as personal care and grooming necessities, and many customers quite naturally assumed the cosmetic Max Factor was the source of both.[6]

Slogans as Trademarks

Slogans are important parts of today's advertising. "Good to the last drop," "When it rains it pours," "Where there's life, there's Bud" are well established and well known as identifiers of Maxwell House coffee, Morton's salt, and Budweiser beer. Other examples include Kellogg Company's "It's gonna be a great day," Canadian Club's "The Best in the House," McDonald's Corporation's "Nobody can do it like McDonald's can," and Eastern Airlines' "We have to earn our wings every day."

Slogans can be established, registered, and protected as trademarks (or service marks) in the same manner as single words or unique designs. In displaying a slogan, the exhibit of "TM" with it, or ® if it is registered, is good practice.

One of the most famous slogans is "Put a Tiger in Your Tank!," which was used worldwide during the 1960s and early 1970s by affiliates of Exxon Corporation in connection with gasoline sales. The slogan is a famous trademark not only in English but in several foreign languages as well. Several companies have attempted a free ride on the goodwill of the "Tiger" slogan by replacing "Tiger" or "Tank" or both with their own animals or containers or products. Because the slogan is so well established as an Exxon property, Exxon has been successful in protecting its rights to exclusive use.

Design Trademarks

The same criteria apply to symbols or graphic trademarks as apply to word trademarks. They must be distinctive and point to a single source. A design trademark has at least one advantage over a word mark. Assuming it is unique, a good design mark can overcome language barriers in identifying a particular product or service.

Design marks may vary from abstractions to simple use of

geometric shapes. Many incorporate several colors. They may also incorporate letters, words, or numbers in regular typefaces or in original designs. Practically no subject of nature—animal, vegetable, or mineral—has been immune from exploitation as a design trademark.

Creating a design of pattern and color to serve as a trademark should be done by professionals skilled in trademark design. The "home grown" variety almost invariably lacks artistry and usually falls far short of fulfilling the various functions of a trademark, functions a professional trademark designer weighs carefully.

Color in Trademarks

It is not possible to establish exclusive use of any color. Everyone has equal rights to colors, with but one provision: colors may not be used in the same general pattern or design used in the trademark of another if the result would be confusing similarity. Particular designs or patterns using specific colors can be registered as trademarks.

Some localities have restrictions or requirements on the use of certain colors that might have some effect on the intended use. There may be restriction on signs that are predominantly red or green when located near traffic signals, for example.

Geometric Shapes

Circles, triangles, squares, ovals, rectangles, and other geometric forms appear as basic designs for hundreds of trademarks. As with colors, trademark protection is afforded for a graphic combination that is unique and cannot be confused with a geometric shape used by someone else on similar goods.

"Logotype" Trademarks

A logotype ("logo") is a trademark consisting of a company or product name in a special design. The term *logotype* has no special or unusual significance in trademark management. It is used from time to time in trade literature with reference to a trademark in unique graphic form.

Words that cannot pass muster for trademark registration might be registerable if a unique design is used (i.e., a logotype). Almost every city has one or more stores named "Pipe and Tobacco Shop." As an owner, you can distinguish yours from others by having "Pipe and Tobacco Shop" drawn in a unique ("logo") style. It would not do simply to pick out a standard style of type different from that used by competition, since the various standard typefaces are available to anyone. A commercial artist could do the job. By displaying your new logo on your shop window or door, and applying it to the pouches of your tobacco blends and on the flannel bags in which your finest pipes are sold, on matchbook covers, and on packages of pipe cleaners, you may well establish trademark rights to the logo and register it.

A trademark that is both a unique word and a unique design is doubly protected. Exxon, for example, is a coined, unique word, and in its logotype form is a unique design embodying interlocked X's. The word "Exxon" in regular typeface, in its logotype form, and in the special style of the X's are all registered trademarks.

What Cannot Be Protected as a Trademark

Almost any word or design may be *used* as a trademark. Under the Lanham Act, however, specific types of words and designs are excluded from trademark protection and are incapable of being registered. The list falls broadly into two groups: (1) words or designs that are common property and cannot be removed from the language or art as exclusive property of an individual or company, and (2) words or designs that are immoral, deceptive, or fraudulent.

More specifically, words or designs that fall under the following categories cannot be protected as trademarks:

Generics   Any word that is generic for a type of product cannot be registered as a trademark for that product. "Bicycle," "candle," "arrow," "pencil," "stove," "window," and so on are available for common use on such items.

The flag, coat of arms, or other insignia or their imitations of any federal, state, or municipal government in the United States or abroad.

Words that primarily are merely surnames   The use of sur-names and their possible protection as trademarks are discussed earlier in this chapter.

Names of cities, countries, states, or counties or other geo-graphical locations that merely describe the origin of the product or service, or that are used intentionally to deceive as to source.

The name, portrait, or signature of a living person, except through the person's written consent, or of a deceased U.S. presi-dent during the lifetime of his widow except with her written consent.

Words, phrases, or designs that disparage or falsely suggest a connection with persons living or dead, institutions, beliefs, or national symbols or bring them into contempt or disrepute.

"Immoral, deceptive, or scandalous" designs, words, or phrases   The Lanham Act does not define the three words here quoted. Certainly the public concept of what is moral or immoral, or what is scandalous or not, has changed drastically since the act was written. It would be sheer folly, however, to adopt as a trade-mark any word or design that might offend the sensibilities of any segment of the population, despite liberation of parts of the lan-guage or art heretofore banned in polite society.

"Deceptive" words or phrases include, but are not necessarily limited to, those that falsely characterize the product, as distinct from arbitrary or suggestive marks. "Wisconsin" in the brand name of a cheese made in Arkansas would be deceptive as to the origin. "Golden" could be deceptive for a product having neither the color nor the metal nor the value. A mark may be deceptive if it is laudatory or is an exaggeration. "Best in the World," "Lasts For-ever," or "Trouble Free" certainly may be vulnerable as possibly deceptive marks because they are laudatory or are exaggerations.

The Lanham Act makes no provision for registering marks that identify processes, as for example a unique process for cleaning carpets or a special or unique chemical or physical process used in raw material conversion. If a service accompanies the process, a mark for the allied service might be registerable. Or if a product is the result of the process, a trademark for the product might be established. Either mark could then be used in connection with promoting the process, giving some measure of unique identity to the process itself.

Weak and Overworked Trademarks

In contrast to strong trademarks that are unique and so distinctive as to deserve and receive broad protection, weak trademarks lack distinctiveness and are entitled to very narrow protection or none at all. Weak trademarks generally are common words applied as brand names in a manner that describes the product (Metal), indicates a characteristic or benefit of its use (Easy, Economy), or implies superior qualities (Magic). Weak trademarks are used by hundreds of manufacturers for a wide variety of products.

Simply misspelling a common word usually does nothing to strengthen it as a trademark, or to give it any particular distinction. The word "Easy" and variations such as "E–Z," "EAS–E," and "EZY" is a typical example. A recent Trademark Index of *Thomas Register* includes over 350 entries of "Easy" and its variations, of which "E–Z" is most common. Another example is Clear, Klear, and Kleer, constituting nearly 150 brands in the list.[7]

Weak trademarks are virtually impossible to establish and protect as the unique property of one owner. Such marks lack distinction as indications of source. Also, because so many weak trademarks are identical or nearly so in spelling or sound, it is difficult to distinguish one product from another. Mini-Flex, Nu-Life, and Superlite, for example, are all used by more than one manufacturer.

The spelling of a trademark is not the sole criterion of similarity. The sound of it is important also. When you speak of "Easy Lift" or "EZ–Lift" (both have multiple listings in the *Thomas Register*), how do you distinguish between the two without elaboration?

You would have plenty of company if your inclination is to brand your product with as descriptive a word as possible (Clear, Dry, Green, Wood), or to imply superior qualities (Ace, Diamond, Giant, Excel, Super), or to indicate use (Aqua, Electro, Lock, Protecto, Thermal). Table 3 is a list of words or word segments used as brands or as the first word or prefix of a brand. Each of these words, or the word and its variations where more than one spelling is shown, appear 100 times or more in a recent edition of the

Table 3: Weak and Overworked Trademarks

Aero
Air
All
Aluma, Alumi
American
Aqua
Astra, Astro
Auto
Big
Black
Blu, Blue
Chem, Kem
Chroma, Chrome,
  Chrom, Chromo,
  Kroma, Krome,
  Krom, Kromo
Clean, Klean,
  Kleen
Clear, Klear, Kleer
Color
Cool, Kool
Diamond
Double, Dubl
Dri, Dry
Dual, Duo
Dura, Duri, Duro
Dyna
Easi, Easy, E–Z,
  EZY
Econo, Economy
Electra, Electric,
  Electro, Lectra,
  Lectro
Ever

Excel, Excello,
  Excelo, X–L
Flex, Flexa, Flexi,
  Flexo
Flo, Flow
Floor, Flor
Form
Gold, Golden
Green
Grip
Hand, Handee,
  Handi, Handy
Hi, High, Hy
Hydra, Hydri,
  Hydro
Ideal
Imperial
Insta, Instant
Iso
Jet
Lady
Light, Lite
Liqua, Liqui,
  Liquid
Little
Lo, Low
Load
Lock, Lok
Long
Lub, Lubra, Lubri
  Lubro
Luster, Lustra,
  Lustre, Lustro
Magi, Magic

Magna, Magne,
  Magni
Mark
Master
Metal, Met–L
Micra, Micro,
  Mikro
Mini
Mono
Moto, Motor
Multa, Multi
Neo
Neu, New, Nu
No, Non
Old, Olde
Para
Perma, Permi,
  Permo
Plast, Plasta, Plasti,
  Plasto
Poly
Porta, Porto
Power, Powr
Press
Protecta, Protecto,
  Protex
Quick, Quik, Qwik,
  Kwik
Rapid, Rapi, Rapido
Ray
Ready, Redi, Redy
Red
Rol, Roll
Rota, Roto

Royal

Saf, Safe, Safe–T, Safety,

San, Sana, Sani, Sano

Seal, Seal–a, Seal–o

Select, Selecta, Selecto, Selectra, Selectro

Serva, Serve, Servi, Servo

Shur, Sure

Silver

Sno, Snow

Speed, Speedi, Speedy

Spray

Sta, Stay

Star

Steel

Sun

Super, Supra

Syn

Tela, Tele

Therm, Therma, Thermi, Thermo

Tough, Tuf, Tuff, Tuffy

Trans

Tri, Triple

Tru, True

Twin

Ultra

Uni

Vac, Vaca, Vacu

Van

Vara, Vari

Vel, Velva, Velve, Velvi

Verso, Versi

Vibra, Vibro

Victor, Victory

West, Western

White

Wood

Trademark Index of *Thomas Register* as being in use by different manufacturers.

If qualification for this list had been twenty-five or more entries in *Thomas Register*, rather than 100, the number of entries would have approached 400. This sampling illustrates three points. First, almost every common word or variation of it that describes a product, praises it, or indicates its use appears as a brand or part of a brand on someone's product. Second, it underscores the importance of an availability search (discussed in Chapter 5) to avoid duplicating someone else's trademark. Third, unique brands or trademarks are difficult to find and require work to develop if the product is to stand out from the crowd.

A Truly "Super" Brand?

Perhaps the most overworked brand of all is "Super." *Thomas Register* lists nearly 900 "Super," "Supre," and "Supra" brands. The Trademark Register of the United States lists over 2,100 registrations of "Super" and "Super" combinations.

The listings of the Trademark Register show "Super" to be used most frequently for "Cutlery, Machines, and Tools, and Parts Thereof" (U.S. Class 23). Some 130 Super brands are registered in this class alone.

When you or your advertising agency comes up with a really super idea, it may not, after all, be the basis for a really "super" brand, unless you want plenty of company.

5

Creating
a New Trademark

There is no easy or magic formula for creating a mark that is unique, simple, distinctive, and memorable. Such an accomplishment requires thought and time. The best tools are pencil, paper, and perspiration—very rarely does an outstanding trademark result from a flash of genius. Creating a graphic (design) trademark, with or without words, letters, or numbers, presents special problems. The services of a professional designer are strongly recommended, as discussed in Chapter 11.

One of the primary problems in creating a trademark is time. Too often, the research department comes up with an attractive new product, sometimes representing years of work, ready for the market. What to call it is almost invariably the last consideration. "We need a name today, or better yet, yesterday."

Under the pressures of time, companies too often adopt a trademark that is hastily conceived; they give little thought to trademark functions and characteristics, and most important of all, they do not determine whether the mark is already in use by someone else. Hasty trademark adoption can prove to be a most costly error. A company prints labels and packages, prepares promotional material, and ships the product, usually at a cost of thousands of dollars, only then to find that the trademark it rushed into being infringes on the mark of another company. An expensive lawsuit threatens. The head of one trademark search organization has estimated that each year a thousand trademark infringement lawsuits are in progress in the United States, most of which probably could have been avoided had the defendants bothered to determine existing trademarks. *Never can it be assumed that a newly created trademark is unique and clever enough to be free of conflict and available for immediate use.* A professional search for trademark availability is by far the most important step in the procedures suggested here after candidate marks are selected.

Developing the *right* trademark can take months or even years. With luck, it might be done in a few weeks, but a quickie that is also a winner is indeed a rare exception. Standard Oil Company (New Jersey) spent more than five years of concerted effort to develop Exxon and to ensure exclusive rights to it. The chairman of the trademark committee for a large pharmaceutical company stated that they expect trademark development for a new proprietary drug to require two years on the average.

To minimize the time problem, people involved in trademark development and administration should keep abreast of what the research department is doing, try to anticipate the need for a trademark, and start working on it well ahead of the ultimate need. If the product should die on the vine, some time may have been wasted, but that is preferable to having a new product sitting idle awaiting baptism, or being branded with an inappropriate mark hastily conceived.

Who should be involved in developing a new trademark? Many companies turn the problem over to their advertising agencies or to a marketing or design consultant. Yet the final choice rests within the company organization. The executives and managers of departments who must make the product a success should have a voice in the selection. Top management, too, should at least be kept informed. Frequently, new trademark development is the responsibility of a trademark committee. These management methods are discussed in Chapters 8 and 9.

Trademark creation is not a job for trademark counsel, as counsel usually is more concerned with the legal strength of the mark than with its sales appeal or commercial superiority. Moreover, counsel cannot be expected in most instances to be skilled or trained in marketing objectives, sales strategies, and consumer psychology. Certainly, the advice of counsel should be sought in evaluating proposed marks in terms of their probable legal strengths and the possibility of conflicts or other legal problems. To avoid the advice of counsel could well open the road to legal difficulties.

A degree of secrecy can be very important in trademark development. Even a trivial statement—"We're thinking of calling it Glog"—at the wrong time or place could trigger outright theft of Glog by a zealous competitor or by a trademark pirate. The lack of secrecy also could be an open invitation for unwanted advice or opinions serving primarily to delay the final choice. The name change to Exxon was such a carefully guarded secret that the vast majority of employees were caught by surprise when it was announced.

In searching for a new trademark, it may be tempting to look over a list of well-known and well-established trademarks with the thought of simply adding, deleting, or changing a letter or two to arrive at a new mark. It won't work. The resulting trademark would cause confusing similarity, which is prohibited by trademark law. For example, EXXOM would be confused with EXXON, NABICO with NABISCO, or EVERREADY with EVEREADY. Create your own unique trademark rather than attempting a free ride on the goodwill of an existing mark.

Steps in Creating a Trademark

An orderly and objective approach to trademark selection and development will save time, and the chances for success are superior to those of a shotgun approach. The first step is to become thoroughly familiar with the functions of trademarks and the characteristics and types as discussed in the two previous chapters. Keep in mind the objectives the new mark is expected to fulfill. Progression may then be somewhat along the following lines. Obviously, not all of these steps apply equally in every situation.

- Become familiar with the new product or service and the marketing plans for it.
- Become familiar with competitive brands and customer buying habits with respect to brands.
- Establish guidelines for the character of the needed trademark.
- Prepare a list of candidate marks.
- Consider possible language problems, foreign and English.

- Select the prime candidates.
- Order a search of the prime candidates by a professional search organization.
- Analyze the professional search.
- Trial market the leading candidates.
- Make your final selection.

No matter how many of the steps you use or omit, the professional search and its analysis are absolute musts.

Familiarize Yourself with the Product

Become generally familiar with the product you are to brand and the general plans for marketing it, particularly if your company is diversified. Trademarks that might be suitable in one line of goods may be quite inappropriate in another. A childish or facetious mark might work well with toys or games but could be quite wrong for a product to be promoted in a dignified and serious manner.

Is the product to be sold from retail shelves where package graphics, brand prominence, and eye appeal are important? How will the brand show up on the package? Is the product to be a salesman's item with product brochures or data sheets? Is it for mass markets having unrestricted demand or for special markets with limited demand? Are foreign markets in its future? While these questions may not have ready answers at this stage, they are considerations that will influence the ultimate choice of a new trademark.

Check Competitive Brands and Customer Practice

Competitive branding of a particular type of product often falls into a discernible pattern. For example, garden fertilizers and chemicals usually have trademarks or trademark segments suggesting agriculture, growth, gardens, greenery, or pest removal. If you elect to ignore the general pattern and try for a brand outside it, you may have a tougher job convincing the buying public that your product is a part of the competitive mix.

Many lines of products are identified by one trademark for the entire line, with the various products within the line identified by generic terms. For example, ORTHO identifies a line of house and garden pesticides made by Chevron Chemical Company. Individual products within the line are labeled generically: Home Orchard Spray, Home Pest Killer, 3–Way Rose and Flower Care, Flying and Crawling Insect Spray, and Chickweed and Clover Control. The line also includes the branded product Weed–B–Gon Lawn Weed Killer.

For products usually identified in this manner, the introduction of a line with a unique brand name for each, rather than generics, might deter sales. Customers might well be inclined to look for the familiar and recognizable label (e.g., "Ant and Roach Killer") instead of relying on an unfamiliar brand such as THUD.

For certain types of industrial products, it may be a futile exercise to develop a brand name for goods purchased almost exclusively on the basis of government or industry specifications. Generic labeling with reference to the specification or standard might be entirely adequate for the particular product and market. In fact, trying to sell a product by brand name could be a detriment when all the purchasing agent cares about is product material strength or performance in relation to reference standards and your reliability.

Establish Guidelines

What type of trademark are you seeking: fanciful, arbitrary, suggestive, or descriptive? Does your company have a preference regarding the number of letters or syllables for its product brands? Are certain initial letters used frequently or consistently? Are some taboo? Are hyphenated words used or preferred?

Set down a few guidelines for the new mark, as for example:

- brand to suggest product use
- one-syllable word, not over six letters
- initial letters G, K, Q, Y, and Z are out
- for mass merchandising; must stand out, be recognizable, memorable, advertisable
- United States now, possible foreign markets later

These guidelines should not be considered hard-and-fast rules, but rather directional assists through the remaining steps.

Prepare a Candidate List

Now comes the hard part—preparing a list of words that may serve as a trademark. Start writing. Put down letter combinations as they come to mind. For word marks, consider using a computer to print various letter combinations. This can be extremely helpful, for within the computerized offerings you may find precisely what you want. On the other hand, much of the computer printout may prove utterly useless, depending on the sophistication of the computer program. However, a computer printout will serve time and again. Although it may not fulfill a need today, it may prove most useful later. This chapter, while based on the pencil-and-paper approach, is adaptable also to the use of computers.

Don't try to evaluate your ideas at this stage. Let one combination of letters suggest another; rearrange the combinations. Arrange alphabetically your list of thirty, forty, or one hundred ideas. Put the list aside overnight or for a week or a month. Before attacking the list again, review the considerations suggested in the first three steps. Then evaluate your ideas, crossing out the obvious misfits. Add new combinations and new ideas. You may choose to let the list mellow again for a few days and then repeat the culling/revision process. At some point you will arrive at a list of ten to twenty or so leading choices. Do not try at this stage to boil it down to the one big prizewinner. There are still too many hurdles to be cleared.

Consider Possible Language Problems

An important consideration for any proposed trademark is its translation or interpretation in foreign languages. A word that is quite innocent and acceptable in English might become derogatory or obscene in another language. Even though a product is to be sold only in an English-speaking country, possible foreign language connotations of the proposed brand should not be ignored. When foreign markets are involved, the language comparison should of course be much broader.

The best comparisons are "living language" studies made by native linguists in the foreign countries of interest. Such "on the scene" experts are familiar with dialects and nuances of interpretation that frequently are unknown to language students who are not natives of the country. Simply to check foreign language dictionaries, or to discuss translations with an acquaintance of foreign origin, while perhaps serving as an initial screening, does not provide the depth of comparison available in the foreign country itself. Large international advertising agencies generally can provide such service. Many of the large design firms who do corporate identity programs are capable of, or have access to, language investigations.

For *initial* screening, consultation with a linguist or foreign language student or examination of foreign language dictionaries may point directly to an undesirable meaning of a proposed trademark, eliminating it from further consideration.

Keep in mind that different languages have different alphabets. The Spanish alphabet has no letter *w*. Italian has no *j*, *k*, *w*, *x*, or *y*. This may pose no serious problem, unless the intent is to enter a largely Italian market with a product called WJXYK. The point is not to become boxed in with a brand name that would be troublesome to a particular ethnic group making up a significant part of the intended market.

Do not expect to find a nice foreign word that you can use as a trademark and register as such if, in English, the word is the generic term for the product. You might choose to brand your new paint with the Italian word *pittura,* but it could not be registered as a trademark because it means "paint" in English.

Insofar as English is concerned, one consideration you should not overlook is the sound of a brand on the telephone, or in radio or TV advertising. Consider DREEZ, for example. Despite spelling it out in a vocal exchange, customers will look for BREEZE, because D and B sound too much alike. Similarly, V and B are sometimes difficult to distinguish over the telephone or radio. While there is no crime in spelling out a product name, the exercise "D as in dog, R, E, E, Z, no final E" is laborious and could distract from the name itself.

Many unique trademarks become garbled or lost in radio advertisements. The commercials are taped or recorded in studios designed for acoustic excellence, and on replay in the studio the trademark is clear and discernible. But over the air, received on pocket transistors or car radios, or on kitchen radios competing with a dishwasher, the product name often goes down the drain. If the *sound* of your product name is important, consider it under adverse as well as ideal conditions.

Select the Prime Candidates

As a result of the first five steps, you now have a list of a dozen or more possible marks. At this stage (if it hasn't been done earlier), the list should be reviewed with others responsible for marketing and promoting the product. Their opinions are important. It may be politic to go as high as the president or chief executive officer of the company. Few executives like surprises, and the appearance on the market of a brand name about which they were not consulted, or at least informed, could have unfortunate results.

During this review, obtain opinions as to order of preference for the candidate marks. Some marks may well be rejected out of hand by persons in high authority. List the surviving candidates in order of preference based on the combined opinion. It might be advisable to circulate the composite opinion to all who were consulted. Ranking the choices certainly is not a crucial step, but it may prove to be a useful reference later if two or more candidate marks prove equally available.

Order a Professional Search of Availability

Every proposed new trademark or trade name should be searched to determine its availability—whether it is in use and the extent of its use—*before* it is adopted. Of all the steps suggested here, this is perhaps the most important. When you, in all innocence, duplicate someone else's trademark, the law is clearly on the side of the original user. The best of intentions is no excuse.

There are three firms in the United States (of which the author is aware) that conduct trademark availability searches.

TCR Service, Inc.
P.O. Box 936
Englewood Cliffs. N.J. 07632

Thomson and Thomson
120 Fulton Street
Boston, Mass. 02109

Trademark Services Corp.
747 Third Avenue
New York, N.Y. 10017

These organizations have on file hundreds of thousands of words and designs used as trademarks and trade names. The files are constantly updated through almost daily reference to hundreds of trade journals and directories, telephone directories, advertisements, and other publications as well as to the notices and files of the United States Patent and Trademark Office.

The services offered by these search organizations are varied, ranging from an all-out search (e.g., is THUD used by anyone, anywhere, for anything?) to a limited search for a specified application in a specific class of goods (e.g., is THUD used as a trademark for insecticides in international class 5?).

The searches cover use only in the United States. (For foreign searches, see Chapter 10.) Fees for a search are generally modest. Compared with the costs that could arise if a mark were adopted without a search, the expenditure is negligible. Usually, a professional search requires from two to four weeks to complete.

An example of a search report is shown in Appendix 2A. The candidate mark is ZAM for car polish made by ZAM Industries. While both ZAM and ZAM Industries are works of fiction created specifically as examples, the search report lists actual trademarks and trade names.

Despite your best efforts and those of the professional search organization, no search can guarantee 100 percent disclosure of identical or similar marks. Many trademarks and trade names in use are not registered or are used in a very limited manner or are so recently adopted as to escape the notice of professional searchers.

An in-house initial screening You can conduct your own limited search of word trademarks for an *initial* screening of your ideas. This will give you an approximate but not conclusive idea of whether your proposed marks seem to be unique, or whether you might be headed for conflict. By eliminating from your list the obvious potential troublemakers, you present to the professional searcher a list of candidate trademarks with a better chance of success.

Some may consider unwarranted the cost of the time devoted to this in-house screening. It might be less expensive to go directly to the professional search firm with all candidate marks. Nevertheless, a trademark administrator can collect several lists of existing trademarks, and in a relatively short time—a matter of an hour or so—obtain an indication of whether candidate marks may be headed for trouble. Under no circumstances should the in-house screening be substituted for the professional search.

Several types of references are available in various company offices and in public libraries. Use as many as you can find, as none is all-inclusive. There is no single list of all trademarks and trade names.

The most comprehensive list of *registered* trademarks (outside the U.S. Patent and Trademark Office) is *The Trademark Register of the United States.*[1] It lists by classes of goods and services the trademarks currently registered in the United States. In using this reference, search not only in the class or classes of goods or services of immediate interest, but also in those classes related by nature of the goods and by the type of use or by channels of trade. For each listed trademark, *The Trademark Register* shows the date of registration and registration number, but not the owner or the specific goods or services, nor are design trademarks illustrated. The professional search usually discloses this information, or a copy of the registration can be obtained by writing to the U.S. Patent and Trademark Office.

The *Thomas Register of American Manufacturers* includes a large section, "The American Trademark Index," which lists trademarks and indicates the type of product and the name and address of the manufacturer.[2]

Telephone directories of large metropolitan areas, both the alphabetical listings and the classified sections, can be culled for names similar to those of your candidates. Appendix 3 lists several additional sources of trademark and trade name information.

In conducting your initial screening search, check not only the exact spelling of your candidate marks, but spellings that might sound or look like yours. For example, you are considering CRAX for a new game or toy. Look not only for CRAX, but also for CRACK, CRACKS, KRAX, KRACKS, CLAX, CLACKS, QRAX, and so on.

Let us say that in your search you discover KRAX for a cement patching mixture as the only name similar to CRAX. Because the goods and channels of trade are quite different, your use of CRAX on a toy or game is not automatically eliminated by KRAX. In fact, barring other disclosures of similar names through a professional search, CRAX appears to be a promising candidate at this stage. On the other hand, you discover KRACK for a line of toy trucks, toy road graders, and the like. Your chances for CRAX are practically eliminated because the KRACK toys would be sold in the same outlets and store departments as CRAX. Further search and alternative action may be warranted, as discussed later, if CRAX is your prime choice.

A nonprofessional search of proposed design trademarks is much more difficult, much less informative, and much less certain than an in-house search of proposed word trademarks. At best, it can only be hit or miss, by leafing through the advertising pages of trade journals and business publications, or volumes such as *Thomas Register,* studying the various design trademarks displayed therein. The most extensive published compilation of design marks is *1979 Trademark Design Register* (see Appendix 3), but this volume is not likely to be found in smaller public libraries.

Evaluation for confusing similarity is also much more difficult with design trademarks than word trademarks. If the proposed design is identical to an existing graphic, then there can be no doubt as to confusion. But the "confusing similarity" of two pieces of art often is a matter of minute detail, similar proportions, or similar use of colors. Design work should be placed in the hands of professional designers and design searches in the hands of professional search organizations.

Analyze the Professional Search

The professional search report simply provides information. It does not offer legal opinion as to possible conflicts or as to whether your candidate names can be registered as trademarks. A trademark attorney should evaluate the report in terms of possible conflict of your candidate marks with the marks shown in the report. The attorney may find all of your gems are too close for comfort to existing marks. According to one trademark search authority, some 80 to 85 percent of proposed trademarks submitted for search fall by the wayside because either the marks are in use or they are generic and cannot be registered as trademarks.

It is therefore highly probable that a search will disclose marks that apparently conflict with one or more of your prime candidates. However, the search report does not show the *current* use status of the listed marks. Many marks established with the best of intentions and that show up in searches have been abandoned because the products on which they were used didn't make the grade. Consequently, further checking into the present status of marks that seem to be in your way may be warranted.

One way to find out whether a mark is still in use is to write to the company owning the mark, asking for product and price information for the particular brand in question. The reply may show the mark still in use. If the mark is not in use, is it for sale? If you opt to check further into whether the owner might be interested in selling the mark, you would be well advised to do so through your attorney, "acting on behalf of a client." It is amazing how a dormant trademark, sometimes one even forgotten by its owner, will take on a high and ridiculous price when interest in it is expressed. This is particularly true if it becomes known that the source of the inquiry is a well-known or a large firm. Sometimes, however, the time and cost of such further checking could well exceed the time and cost of starting over, preparing a new list of candidate marks, and ordering new searches.

Comments regarding the ZAM search report are included in Appendix 2B.

Trial Market the Marks

Surviving from the search are two or three of your candidates, all of which appear equally good to you. Trial marketing may show which is the best, or whether none is any good. It is beyond the scope of this book to discuss trial marketing procedures and analysis. Retain a marketing consultant to do the job if your company is not staffed to do it.

Make Your Final Selection

No elaboration is necessary for this step, except that you should make certain all who will be involved in the success of the new product with its new trademark are aware of it and agree with the selection before it is announced publicly.

The task of trademark selection often is frustrating and sometimes exasperating. It may be helpful to refer to other treatments of the subject. For example, attorneys Campbell and Cohen, in *Trademark Selection and Protection*, treat the availability search and its analysis in considerably more detail than is done here.[3] They also cite many court cases involving selection and protection. Sidney Diamond, in *Trademark Problems and How to Avoid Them*, devotes Chapter 2 to "How to Choose a Trademark."[4] The United States Trademark Association's *Trademark Selection—The Management Team Method* presents a verbatim panel discussion of the subject at its 1960 annual meeting.[5] The USTA also has several short articles on the subject.*

Despite Your Best Efforts, You Still Might Lose

If you have done everything possible to come up with a unique name or trademark, the odds are greatly in your favor that you are home free and clear. But not certain. The uncertainty stems from several factors. First, in the United States, a trademark must be put into use before it may be registered, and the first user gets the trademark, whether registered or not. Another company may beat you to the mark by a matter of a day, and because it is a new mark, it will not show up in searches. Second, trademarks

---

*BBDO Research Services, of BBDO International, Inc., 583 Madison Avenue, New York, N.Y. 10017, published in January 1981 *Developing and Testing New Names for Brands and Products.*

established through use are protected by law even if not registered with the U.S. Patent and Trademark Office, and, because the use may be relatively minor, such marks may elude the searches. Finally, because trade names, trademarks, and service marks, both registered and unregistered, number in the millions, some are bound to escape the searcher's best efforts.

You launch your new trademark with suitable fanfare. Shortly afterward, you receive a letter or call from the owner of an identical or similar mark, hinting at infringement (or possibly stronger language) because of confusing similarity. Again, if you did your homework, the odds of this happening are small, but the point is that it can and does happen. Your trademark attorney may be able to convince the owner's trademark attorney that the channels of trade are different, or that the goods really aren't that similar after all. Perhaps your adversary is willing to sell the disputed trademark. On the other hand, you may have no choice but to apologize and withdraw the new mark you developed so carefully.

A Word about Brand-Name Contests

Frustration in coming up with a suitable brand name sometimes leads to the idea "Let's have an employee contest for a brand name!"

Don't. Worse yet, don't throw the search for a brand open to the public.

Every contest must have a winner. The chances are slim indeed that the entered names would resemble what you are looking for. Consequently, either you are stuck with a contest winner not to your liking, or you declare a winner and forget the whole thing. Later, when you brand the product with a name of your own development, you may have a disgruntled employee to cope with.

Or you file and forget the entered names after declaring a winner that you have no intention of using. Later, you develop a name that may in some remote way resemble one of the contest entries. You are now in trouble, because the contestant believes you copied his or her idea.

Remember, too, that every possible contest finalist must be

searched if you intend to use one of them. Unless your employees are extremely clever, the chances are quite high that all the proposed names will fall by the wayside upon search and analysis.

A public brand-name contest, on the other hand, may be a good way to announce and introduce your new product. Weigh the associated problems and consequences carefully. The problems associated with employee contests are multiplied many times in a public contest. Unless you are willing to face those problems, stay away from contests.

Trademark Ownership and Registration

Ownership of a new trademark should be established immediately upon its selection, in order to benefit from the exclusive rights provided by ownership. Even if the mark is intended for a product not quite ready for marketing, do not wait until the marketing plans are set and the product is ready for distribution. Delay could be costly. Good new trademarks are hard to find, and it is quite possible someone else could be establishing first use and ownership of the same mark or one confusingly similar to it. If there is a delay of even a few weeks, availability searches should be updated to make certain the selected new mark remains free of possible conflict (see Chapter 5).

In the United States, trademark *ownership* stems from *first use*. Ownership entitles the owner to exclusive use of the mark for the type of product on which it is applied and for so long as it is used. Unless the mark becomes famous, ownership usually does not prevent someone else from using the same mark on unrelated products or products moving through different trade channels. Trademark *registration*, on the other hand, is the government's formal recognition of ownership, issued when satisfactory evidence of use is supplied. Registration in the United States is a possible consequence of trademark ownership, rather than the method of establishing it. The advantages provided by registration weigh heavily in its favor, even though ownership is established by use under common law.

Establishing Ownership
for Federal Trademark Registration

Any person may establish ownership in a trademark and file for federal registration. However, consultation with a trademark attorney or other person authorized to practice in trademark cases is strongly recommended. A professional skilled in trademark matters knows the forms to use, the documents to supply, the records to keep, and the procedures to follow, as well as steps to take if problems arise. The road to federal trademark registration is not always smooth. The following paragraphs summarize most of the considerations involved. For details of filing procedures and forms, see the Patent and Trademark office's *Trademark Rules of Practice.*[1]

To establish ownership for purposes of U.S. registration, the trademark must first be used. Exactly what constitutes "use" and how much "use" is sufficient for trademark registration are not easily specified because of various rulings in a wide variety of situations. It is clear, however, that "use" means use in commerce, and the commerce must be between the states, or between territories of the United States and foreign countries. Commerce solely within a single state does not serve for federal registration purposes. "Use" must be a normal business use—either a sale, lease, or shipment of the branded product. Earlier or concurrent use of a trademark outside the United States is not a basis for establishing ownership rights in the United States.

The sale, lease, or shipment may be arranged specifically for federal registration purposes—a "qualifying" or "token" use. This is an accepted and legal practice if it is a bona fide commercial transaction. In discussing this form of use, Albert Schwartz writes, "The token sale or single use in commerce, often known as 'token use,' has come to be a widely accepted method of establishing use prior to filing a trademark application while avoiding large expenditures in promoting marks before their registerability can be determined." As a further qualifying consideration, he then quotes the Trademark Trial and Appeal Board:

There are, however, certain restrictions or limitations on this practice, namely, . . . that these shipments not be inter-company transactions for the purpose of company experimentation and research, that these shipments or sales have the color of bona fide transactions, and most important of all, that these shipments be accompanied or followed by activity or circumstances which would tend to establish a continuing effort or intent to continue such use and place the product so shipped on the market on a commercial scale.[2]

Among actual uses held by various court rulings to be *insufficient* in the United States are publicizing a trademark through advertising, listings in trade directories or buyers' guides, product brochures, price lists, and training manuals, ordering labels, display on coupons redeemable for the product, and unsolicited shipments (in this particular case totaling $20) to different dealers with no intent to make public use of the mark.[3] On the other hand, advertising or marketing tests have been held to be bona fide continued use of a trademark after the initial sale.

In arranging a token sale or shipment, the customer cannot be an out-of-state branch of the company or a relative. It is important to document the transaction fully, including the date of first use. Also, photograph the package label displaying the trademark. The package label need not be final finished art, but may be drawn specifically for this purpose. Moreover, it is possible to use for the shipment a product answering the same description and purpose as the product on which the mark ultimately will be applied. Through such token use, a mark can be established for registration prior to full production of a new product.

First Use of a Service Mark

"Use" for registration of a service mark may take a somewhat different tack. To qualify for registration as a service mark, the service to which it is applied must be real and not ancillary or incidental to the sale of a product. Thus, for example, operating restaurants, hotels, or motels, selling insurance, counseling on investments, preparing income tax returns, providing advertising and promotional services, or managing and conducting beauty contests are "services." On the other hand, providing operational instructions or product information or assisting with machinery installation and start-up are contingent on the sale of a product and usually are not considered services qualifying for service mark registration.

If the service is offered and conducted between states, the applicable service mark qualifies for federal registration assuming all other requirements for registration are met. Under relatively recent rulings, services offered only within a single state may also qualify for federal registration if they are available to and used by travelers or customers from out of state. Such services might include, for example, a small intrastate chain of automotive repair shops located along an interstate highway, or a restaurant near a state line or an interstate highway. If federal registration of a service mark for such intrastate services is considered desirable, advertising the services in newspapers going out of state or on radio reaching out-of-state audiences has been held to satisfy use in commerce. For registration purposes, keep records of out-of-state customers by means of credit-card sales slips or other forms of customer registration. Further evidence of interstate use of the service could be provided by photographs of the vehicles parked in the service parking lot showing out-of-state license plates.

Ownership without Registration

In the United States, the first user of the mark thereby becomes the owner, and interstate or intrastate sales of a product bearing the trademark will establish use. Use solely within one state, while establishing ownership, is inadequate for federal registration. The mark must be used in interstate commerce if the trademark is to be registered federally.

Documentation of First Use

All transactions involving first use of a trademark should be documented carefully. Purchase orders, shipping documents, and invoices should show the date of the transaction and the product trademark. A photograph of the product package or label or an actual package or label should be included. These documents should be kept as permanent trademark files, as rights to a trademark could be challenged years after first use is established.

Advantages of Registration

Thousands of trademarks are in use without being registered. However, registration of a trademark in the United States has several advantages over reliance on protection by common law. (Common law is unwritten law based on customs or court decisions, as opposed to statute law. Basically, it provides the first user of a trademark a claim to ownership and trademark protection only in the states where it is used, and little else.) Among the principal advantages of registration are the following:

- Registration is *prima facie* evidence of trademark ownership and exclusive rights to use the mark on the goods for which it is registered. If rights to a registered mark are challenged, the burden of evidence is on the challenger.
- Registration is constructive notice of claim of ownership, so that subsequent users cannot claim they had no knowledge of the prior mark.
- Registration domestically may be used as the basis for registration in certain foreign countries.
- The registration may become incontestable in five years. (Exception—if the mark has been or is being used to violate the antitrust law of the United States.)
- Action for infringement can be brought in federal courts. A trademark not federally registered is protected only under the common law of the state in which it is in use.
- Infringement of a registered trademark may cause assessment of triple damages.
- Registration provides a public record for trademark availability searches.

Duration of Registration

Trademark registration in the United States remains in force for twenty years and may be renewed every twenty years provided the mark is used regularly. During the sixth year of the registration, it is necessary to file an affidavit that the mark is still in use, or that nonuse results from special circumstances rather than an intention to abandon the mark. If the affidavit is not filed, registration is canceled.[4]

The Rights and Limits
of Trademark Ownership and Registration

There are hundreds of court decisions concerning the extent of the rights in a trademark by its owner. The rulings range from total exclusivity, that is, total rights in the trademark for use on any type of product or service, to very narrow protection, to no protection at all. The complexities of the subject, of which the following account is a brief generalization, strongly suggest that trademark owners having problems consult with a trademark attorney.

Trademark ownership reinforced by registration protects the owner's exclusive use of the mark on the specific type of product or service on which it is applied. Protection extends also to preventing another's use of a confusingly similar mark on the same products, on products related by characteristics or customary use, and on products that move through the same channels of trade (i.e., products likely to be sold through similar types of outlets or through similar types of merchandising). The test of similarity of trademarks is whether a consumer seeing the marks on similar or different products would either be confused as to product source or quality or would conclude that the products, though different, were from the same origin.

Sometimes a trademark owner can prevent another's use of a confusingly similar mark by establishing proof that customers are likely to be confused. Generally, this requires a well-designed survey and interview with a significant cross section of consumers in one or more typical markets. Several marketing consultant and opinion survey organizations are qualified to conduct such tests.

A strong trademark that has become well established is generally so well recognized by consumers that they would assume common origin of any product on which the mark is used. Consequently, the owner of a strong or famous mark usually is accorded broad trademark protection. Jell-O is so well known that it would be protected for use by its owner, General Foods, on any type of food or beverage, or almost any type of item likely to be sold in a grocery store or supermarket, regardless of the coverage of the registration. If supermarket shoppers were to see Jell-O on soups, dog food, frozen baked goods, or plastic wrapping material, they would almost certainly assume these products to be from the manufacturer of Jell-O gelatin desserts. General Foods would be protected from another's use of Jell-O on these products related either by the nature of the goods or their appearance in the same outlet. The protection very probably would extend even more broadly.

Usually, well-known trademarks such as Jell-O, Nabisco, Kodak, Bostitch, Dacron, Elizabeth Arden, and the like point so specifically to source and quality that it would be foolhardy for other companies to attempt use of these marks on totally unrelated goods. Consumers would still expect the usual source of products so labeled.

The protection afforded weak trademarks is extremely limited in most cases, usually extending only to the specific products on which they are used. As mentioned in Chapter 4, the weakest marks consist of common words used in a manner that describes the product, its quality, or use, and such words are available to all. Although trademark rights to such words may be established through use, these rights are very narrow.

Registration According to Classes of Goods and Services

The goods or services for which use of a mark has been established must be stated in applying for trademark registration. The application form calls for the "common, usual or ordinary name of goods." This is important to the examiner in the U.S. Patent and Trademark Office in determining possible conflicts, in verifying the class of goods (see below) within which the registration will be categorized, in publicizing the application, and for inclusion in the registration certificate. Registration provides protection of the mark for the stated goods or services and usually protects the owner against another's use of the same or similar mark on similar or related goods.

The vast variety of products and services for which trademarks may be registered are categorized in various *classes* primarily as a convenience to governments in recording registrations. To protect a mark adequately, an owner should register a mark within each class covering the products or services for which use of the mark has been established. Registration does not automatically protect the mark for use on all goods or services within the class, but only for the goods stated in the application. Another registration within the same class and for the same mark on unrelated goods might be issued to another owner. Moreover, a particular product might have several uses, and such uses might be categorized in several different classes.

The International Classification System

The classification system used by a majority of governments is the *International Classification of Goods and Services to Which Trade Marks Are Applied.* [5] It consists of thirty-four classes of goods and eight classes of services and is the system now used in the United States. Prior to 1973, the United States had its own system of fifty-two classes of goods and eight of services (see Appendix 4).

Although the International Classification System is used by the majority of governments worldwide, several governments classify goods and services according to their own systems instead. The systems, regardless of origin, are sometimes difficult to fathom. In the International System, "blankets" including "traveling rugs" (flying carpets?) are in Class 24 along with "fabrics," a reasonable association. But "horse blankets" are in Class 18 along with leather goods, umbrellas, whips, harness and saddlery. "Electrically heated blankets" occupy a place in Class 10 with surgical, medical, dental, and veterinary supplies, false teeth, and glass eyes. Out of 34 classes in the Japanese system, six are devoted to beverages and foods or food-associated products, while lumped into a single class are machines, apparatus, and implements for a broad range of applications—physical and chemical, optical, photography, motion pictures, medical, including parts and accessories of these goods as well as photographic materials. Anyone seeking a "key" to these various systems could well be in for several hours of frustration.

Word Titles of the International System

On the next page are the short titles adopted by the United States Patent and Trademark Office for the classes of goods and services of the International System. The list, while indicative of the class into which a particular product or service might fall, is not conclusive as the classification frequently seems to depend on interpretation by the classifier. For example, "Housewares and Glass," Class 21, does not include window glass, which is in Class 19, nor mirrors, which could be in Class 9, 10, 12, 13, or 20, depending on application.

Various types of goods and services making up each of the classes of the International System are listed in *Trademark Rules of Practice*, published by the U.S. Dept. of Commerce Patent and Trademark office, and in *International Classification of Goods and Services to Which Trade Marks Are Applied*. The latter also lists alphabetically a great number of types of goods and services and indicates the class into which each would fall. It is worth mentioning that almost all of the classification systems, although revised from time to time, were developed long before the plethora of new products and technical advances of the past few decades. The detailed International System lists "wireless" and "talking machines" but makes no mention of "radio," "phonograph," "stereophonic systems," or "television." Some of today's products have no earlier counterpart, and it may be difficult to determine the class or classes of goods in applying for registration. The only solution is to determine the class or classes that seem most closely related to the product and file accordingly. A trademark office examiner who believes the class applied for is wrong usually will contact the applicant to make a change.

In the United States, a single application may cover any or all of the goods and/or services falling within several classes, provided commercial use has been established for each of the listed goods or services, and a single certificate of registration may be issued. Or, if the owner files several identical applications, each

Class	Title	Class	Title
	Goods		**Goods** (*continued*)
1	Chemicals	24	Fabrics
2	Paints	25	Clothing
3	Cosmetics and cleaning preparations	26	Fancy goods
		27	Floor coverings
4	Lubricants and fuels	28	Toys and sporting goods
5	Pharmaceuticals		
6	Metal goods	29	Meats and processed foods
7	Machinery		
8	Hand tools	30	Staple foods
9	Electrical and scientific apparatus	31	Natural agricultural products
10	Medical apparatus	32	Light beverages
11	Environmental control apparatus	33	Wines and spirits
		34	Smokers' articles
12	Vehicles		
13	Firearms		**Services**
14	Jewelry	35	Advertising and business
15	Musical instruments		
16	Paper goods and printed matter	36	Insurance and financial
		37	Construction and repair
17	Rubber goods		
18	Leather goods	38	Communication
19	Nonmetallic building materials	39	Transportation and storage
20	Furniture and articles not otherwise classified	40	Material treatment
		41	Education and entertainment
21	Housewares and glass		
22	Cordage and fibers	42	Miscellaneous
23	Yarns and threads		

for a different class, the registrations may be consolidated into one certificate. In both instances the total registration fee is the sum of the fees for filing an application in each class.[6]

An Application Example

A company wishes to register PIX for a complete line of photographic chemicals, equipment and services. Under the International System, the classes primarily involved would be:

Class	For	Class	For
1	chemicals	18	leather gadget bags
9	apparatus—cameras, film, enlargers, etc.	37	camera repair services
11	photographic lighting apparatus other than flash bulbs, which are in Class 9	40	film developing
		41	film rentals
		42	taking wedding pictures, portraits, photos for catalogs, etc.
16	photographs and photo albums		

Forms of Registration

It is good practice to file separate applications for each of the various forms in which a trademark will be used (i.e., in ordinary type, in its special graphic form in black and white, and in its special graphic form in color).

The Principal and Supplemental Registers

Upon registration, a word or symbol passing the tests of a true and distinctive trademark is entered on the Principal Register by the U.S. Patent and Trademark Office. The office considers all applications as seeking registration on the Principal Register unless registration on the Supplemental Register is requested.

The distinction between the two lies in the interpretation of "true and distinctive" trademarks (Principal Register) and words or symbols that lack distinctiveness and fail the test of a true trademark, but through use are "capable of becoming" trademarks (Supplemental Register). Coined words, unique symbols, and suggestive and arbitrary marks usually pass the test of true and distinctive marks and are entered on the Principal Register. This includes service marks, collective marks, and certification marks as well as trademarks.

To qualify for the Principal Register as provided by the Lanham Act, the mark must:

- Function as a trademark as defined by the act
- Have been used in commerce
- Have been affixed to the goods or to displays associated with the goods
- Be submitted by written application with verified facts and payment of filing fees

If a trademark appears to be registerable on the Principal Register, as determined by the U.S. Patent and Trademark Office, it is then published in the *Official Gazette* for opposition. (The *Trademark Official Gazette* is published weekly by the U.S. Patent and Trademark Office and is sold by the Superintendent of Documents, U.S. Government Printing Office, Washington, D.C. 20402. Annual subscription rates are available, or single issues may be purchased.) Any person opposing the registration has thirty days to file an opposition or to request an extension of time.[7] Unless opposition is filed, the registration certificate is issued. Marks on the Supplemental Register are published in the *Official Gazette* only when they are registered. Procedures are available for persons who believe they have been damaged or will be damaged by the registration to file for its cancellation (Lanham Act, Sec. 24).

The Lanham Act also provides for registration on the Supplemental Register of items that cannot qualify for the Principal Register. These may be words lacking distinctiveness but capable of becoming trademarks as determined by the examiner in the U.S. Patent and Trademark Office. Package shapes or graphic designs, labels, surnames, slogans, geographical names, and numbers are not usually considered "true and distinctive" marks but may be capable of becoming trademarks through use. For example, through continued public exposure of a particular package shape or label design, consumers learn to recognize the shape or label design as the identification of a particular product from a particular source, and the shape or label serves a trademark function.

Marks that do not qualify for the Principal Register may be registered on the Supplemental Register providing they have been in use for a year and the use has been exclusive. Although lacking the legal status of marks on the Principal Register, they will show up in trademark searches. A notice of registration may be used with such marks (i.e., the circled ® or "Reg. U.S. Pat. & Tm. Off."), the same as with marks of the Principal Register. Otherwise, they lack the advantages discussed earlier in this chapter under "Advantages of Registration." Through long and continued use, a mark on the Supplemental Register might qualify for registration on the Principal Register.

State Registrations

Each of the states has its own trademark registration system. All but two are based on date of first use, as is the federal system. Alabama and Tennessee do not require a first-use date for registration. A state registration protects the trademark only within that state. With few exceptions, the term is ten years before renewal is necessary.

A state registration might be attractive to a firm operating solely within that state and unable to obtain a federal registration. Some trademarks not qualifying for federal registration might be accepted for state registration. Several states provide strong protection against infringement, and many have strong antidilution laws (see Tiffany Doctrine, following). Trade names, which cannot be registered federally, can be registered in some states. Having both state and federal registration affords companies maximum possible protection of their trademarks within the United States.

State registrations will be uncovered in comprehensive trademark searches.

A state registration cannot prevent a subsequent federal registration for the same mark on the same goods of another manufacturer. However, it might be necessary for the federal registration to exclude rights to the mark within the state where the mark is registered. To establish the date of first use in registering the mark, most states accept the date of first use anywhere, either outside or within the state.

State registrations alone (i.e., without federal registration) are not a basis for displaying a trademark registration notice of the type indicating federal registration. "Trademark Registered" would be an accurate statement, but use of ® or "Reg. U.S. Pat. & Tm. Off." would not if the registrations are state registrations only.

The Tiffany Doctrine—
Protection of Well-known Names
and Antidilution Laws

The Tiffany name is well known for fine jewelry, silver, and other fine merchandise and has been so recognized for well over a century. Many years ago, another company started to use "Tiffany" for motion picture films, and the Fifth Avenue jewelry firm brought suit. The court enjoined the use of "Tiffany" on films, reasoning that the Tiffany name was so well known and distinctive that the public, on seeing the name on films, would be likely to assume some connection with or sponsorship by the New York–based merchant. This ruling, protecting well-known names from exploitation by others, has become known as the Tiffany Doctrine.

Similar court action stopped the use of the Tiffany name on a restaurant and also by a manufacturer of ornamental tile. Much more recently, application of the Tiffany Doctrine stopped the use of "Yale" on flashlights and flashlight batteries because of the well-established and well-recognized use of "Yale" on a variety of locks. Other examples exist in the records.

The Tiffany Doctrine is followed today in most industrialized countries and in many developing countries. Within the United

States, some twenty or so states have incorporated the principles of the doctrine into what are called *antidilution laws*. These laws prohibit another's use of well-known marks even on goods or services totally unrelated to those of the owner of the mark. The purpose of the laws is to protect the well-known name against dilution or erosion. Most famous marks in use in the world today are so protected. To achieve such status, a mark must be used commercially for years until it is firmly ingrained in the public mind for particular goods and their origin. Registration alone does not establish such status.

Exclusivity by Legislation

Various U.S. statutes have established for certain organizations or associations the exclusive rights to use specific names, characters, and designs. Examples listed in *Trademark Rules of Practice* include the following:

The American Legion (name)
Big Brothers of America (name, emblems, seals, badges)
Boy Scouts of America (emblems, badges, descriptive or designating marks, and words or phrases used in carrying out its program)
Disabled American Veterans (name)
Future Farmers of America (name and initials FFA)
Girl Scouts of America (similar to exclusivity for Boy Scouts)
Little League Baseball, Incorporated (name, emblem, seals, and badges)
National Safety Council (name, emblem, seals, badges)
Red Cross (relating to unauthorized use or imitation of the Greek red cross on a white ground, or the words "Red Cross" or "Geneva Cross")
Smokey Bear (character and name)
United States Olympic Association (relating to penalty for improper use or imitation of the emblems of the United States Olympic Association or the words "Olympic," "Olympiad," or "Citius Altius Fortius")
Veterans of Foreign Wars of the United States (name, seals, emblems, badges).[8]

7

Proper Trademark Use and Control

A trademark must be used according to specific rules and managed carefully if its status is to be maintained, its functions served, and its value enhanced. Trademark law requires the owner to control use of a mark, whether used by the owner or by a licensee. Otherwise, the trademark may be lost.

The rules and guidelines in this chapter are not found in statutes as specific statements of "do" or "do not." Rather, they stem from numerous court cases and decisions extending over decades. Basically, their purposes are (1) to specify the use of a trademark so consistently as to eliminate any possible doubts as to product identity, origin, and quality; (2) to prevent general adoption of the trademark as the generic term for the goods on which it is displayed; and (3) to show diligence on the part of the trademark owner in controlling the proper use and display of the trademark.

Inconsistent and careless use can destroy the significance of a mark and any goodwill attached to it. In extreme cases, a mark may be declared the generic term for a type of product, whereby it becomes a part of the common language and loses all trademark significance.

All public and private uses and displays of a trademark must be carefully regulated: advertisements in all media, including radio and television; catalogs, brochures, data sheets, and price lists; displays on packages or directly on products; letterheads, business cards, purchase orders, invoices, envelopes, and other business papers; listings in telephone and trade directories; displays on office buildings, highway signs, or other physical facilities; and displays on company vehicles. No use or exposure can be overlooked.

Proper trademark use within the confines of a company is just as important as outside use, because carelessness inside has a way of traveling outside. A single glaring misuse either inside or outside won't destroy a trademark, so long as steps are taken to prevent repetition. But if misuses are allowed to pass uncorrected, they become precedents for future misuses. Variants of the trademark set in, and through erosion, it eventually becomes something quite different from the original. It is then a trademark out of control. Or worse yet, it begins to take on generic sense, and customers view it as the name for a type of product rather than as a sign or badge indicating a particular product source and quality.

Rules and Guidelines for Word Trademarks

Of the rules and guidelines presented here, any one may be extremely important in a particular situation, so it is difficult to rank one above another. Sidney Diamond states, "The first and most important rule is to use the generic name of the product in association with the trademark."[1] Here it is Rule 2.

Rule 1. Distinguish the trademark in print.

The minimum acceptable distinction is use of an initial capital letter:

Domino sugar
Joy detergent
Swingline stapler

Or, the entire mark may be capitalized:

ZENITH radio and television sets
EVEREADY batteries
THERMOPANE insulating glass

Other acceptable distinguishing methods are use of italics, quotation marks, or boldface type.

> *Coleman* heaters
> "Marcal" tissues
> **Morton** salt

Printing the trademark in a color other than the print color of the surrounding text also will serve to distinguish the mark.

Occasionally, a mark is displayed in all lowercase letters on packages or in advertisements, usually in a unique typeface

---

Table 4: Trademark Use Rules

For word trademarks

1. Distinguish the trademark in print.
2. Use the trademark with the generic term for the product.
3. Show the status of the trademark.
4. Never make a plural of a singular trademark.
5. Do not use a trademark as a possessive or as a verb.
6. Display the form of the trademark consistently.
7. Do not combine trademarks.

For design trademarks

8. Reproduce the graphic form of the trademark precisely.
9. If color is included, use the color consistently.
10. Do not embellish or otherwise modify a graphic trademark.
11. Do not use the graphic outline as a frame for messages or illustrations.
12. Show trademark status.

For all trademarks

13. A company misusing its own trademarks cannot expect others to use them properly.

---

or design. Generally, this is not good practice, as it is difficult or impossible for typists or typesetters working on body copy always to reproduce the mark distinctively. The appearance of "zam car polish"* does not set the mark apart from the words of the text, and invites problems of control and protection, even though ZAM Industries may use "zam" in a unique, all-lowercase form on its packages and in its advertisements.

Rule 2. Use the trademark with the generic term for the product.

Do this at least in its first or most prominent display in an advertisement or on a package. A trademark is a proper adjective and needs a noun (a generic) to modify:

>   Uniflo motor oil
>   ZePel rain/stain repeller
>   Dacron polyester

If the trademark appears frequently in an advertisement, the generics need not follow each appearance. It is advisable, however, to use them more than once in lengthy ads, scattered throughout the text. While no law requires the appearance of the generic, its display is important so that consumers will associate the trademark *with* the generic, rather than think of the trademark *as* the generic.

Generic terms should not be capitalized, as capitalization tends to give them the same significance or status as the trademark, or conversely, the trademark may be reduced to the same status as the generic. While display of generics with initial caps or even in all caps is permissible, the legal requirement is distinctive display of the trademark.

An examination of advertisements with package illustrations or of actual packages shows a wide variety of generic term displays. Many are all caps or initial caps but almost always in type that is smaller than the trademark or in a color less eye-catching than that

---

*ZAM car polish is made by ZAM Industries, a figment of the author's imagination created for purposes of certain examples in this text. An actual counterpart in business today is neither intended nor implied.

of the trademark. The body copy of a General Foods advertisement refers to Sanka® Brand Decaffeinated Coffee with the word "Sanka" in a different type style from the other three words, but of approximately the same size.

A minority of advertisements and package labels display generic terms in all lowercase letters. Obviously, many trademarks survive when used with generics other than all lowercase. However, a statement such as "Zam Improved Car Polish, Body Cleaner and Rust Remover in its New Easy to Use Emulsified Form" tends to obscure the trademark or lose it entirely in an overabundance of capitalized generics. This example is typical of statements appearing in some advertisements.

Certain types of products are so well known to the public that the mention of one of the product brands automatically suggests the applicable generic terms even though it is not stated. The mention of Ford, Chevrolet, Plymouth, Jeep, or Volkswagen conjures but one type of product. Similarly, Kent, Chesterfield, Camel, Winston, Parliament, Tareyton, Marlboro. The generic term is understood and its omission does not necessarily endanger the trademark.

Rule 3. Show the status of the trademark.

If—and only if—the trademark is registered with the U.S. Patent and Trademark Office, display the circled R (®) with it:

Kodar®

This applies equally to trademarks, service marks, collective marks, and certification marks entered in either the Principal Register or the Supplemental Register.

Instead of the circled R, other forms of notice may be used to indicate trademark status. For example, an advertisement of Rolls-Royce Motors, Inc., uses this form of trademark notice in a concluding statement:

The names "Rolls-Royce" and "Silver Shadow" and the mascot, badge and radiator grille are registered trademarks as are the Bentley name, mascot and badge.

The circled R does not appear in the Rolls-Royce advertisement.

Trademark status sometimes is indicated by means of a footnote in an advertisement or on a label: ZAM* (at the first or most prominent display of the mark) and the footnote "*ZAM is a registered trademark," or "*Reg. U.S. Pat. & Tm. Off."

Where the mark appears more than once on a package or on a product or in an advertisement, the circled R or other acceptable form of registration notice need not appear with each display of the trademark. A single appearance within the total layout serves the purpose. Often, in lengthy or wordy advertisements, the ® is displayed unnecessarily with every mention of the trademark. According to William Borchard, "A lighter touch in the sprinkling of ® symbols may actually improve the strength of trademark rights."[2]

Many companies publish public relations periodicals, some form of house organ, or other types of literature available to the general public. Several trademarks owned by the company may be mentioned in the various articles making up the publication. A single statement, usually placed in the masthead box, is adequate announcement of the status of the trademarks: "ZAM, ZOC, COZ, and THUD are registered trademarks of ZAM Industries." Trademark status may be treated similarly in technical publications, if products are mentioned by brand, by means of a footnote.

Company correspondence frequently mentions products by

brand name. Unless the correspondence is to be distributed broadly by means of copies and is in the nature of a promotional piece, trademark status need not be indicated. An initial capital letter for the trademark is adequate. Use of a trademark notice may distract from the business message.

If a word or symbol is being used as a trademark that is not registered, the initials TM indicating claim to ownership may be used in the same manner as ®:

Fuel Boss™

Similarly, SM may be used to indicate a claim to ownership of unregistered service marks:

The American Express Card. Don't leave home without it.
_{SM}

There are no specifications for the size or type style of ®, nor of TM or SM, nor the position with respect to the trademark. The circled R should not be located in a manner suggesting trademark registration for words that are not registered parts of the mark. In the Flexon 766 example, the circled R is positioned to apply to the word only, as the numbers are a grade designation not part of the trademark:

Flexon® 766

Although the display of trademark status is not a legal requirement, the display of ® or other form of registration notice may have legal ramifications, as explained in Chapter 6. Many regis-

tered trademarks appear without any form of notice. Some designers object to the notice because in their opinion the inclusion of
®, TM, or SM upsets design balance or graphic purity. At least
one designer, however, has styled the circled R to blend with the
overall style of the trademark:

Display of trademark status is good practice indicating a claim
to ownership and diligence in controlling the mark. It serves, too,
as a "hands off" notice to others who may be searching for a good
new trademark. Some companies use the word "brand" after each
of their trademarks to emphasize trademark status, in the manner
of SANKA® Brand mentioned earlier. JELL-O® Brand Desserts,
SCOTCH® Brand Magic Transparent Tape, and LEGO® Brand
Pre School Building Sets are further examples of such uses.

The symbol Ⓤ indicates kosher products and services that
have been rabbinically supervised under contractual agreement. It
is a form of "OU," the registered certification mark of the Kosher
Certification Service of the Union Orthodox Jewish Congregations
of America (the "Orthodox Union"). The appearance of "P" next to
the circled U indicates kosher for Passover. The circled U has no
legal status as a trademark notice.

Improper registration notice   Just as it is important to know
when to use a registration notice, it is equally important to know

when not to do so. There are basically four situations in which display of ® or other form of notice indicating U.S. registration is improper and such use could lead to trouble.[3] The owner could lose all rights in the trademark, including the right to get an injunction against an infringer.

1. Use of a notice with a mark that is not registered. Moreover, application for registration is not a basis for using a registration notice—the registration must have been issued.

2. Display of the notice in a manner or location that could be construed as applying to unregistered words or symbols as well as to the registered trademark.

3. Display of the notice with a registered trademark used on goods or services not specified in the registration, even though the goods or services may be related.

REYNOLON®
Shrink Film
PACKAGING

Scotchban®
PAPER PROTECTOR

Examples of good trademark practice: an indication of registration status, and the generic terms for the products on which the marks are applied.

4. For trademarks registered in a special graphic form, a registration notice should not be used with some other graphic form of the mark not included in the registration. Frequently, a word mark is registered in block letters. The registration is then considered to cover all other forms of display, and use of a registration notice is permissible with the other forms.

Rule 4. Never make a plural of a singular trademark.

Many companies offer various grades or models of product bearing the same trademark. It is incorrect trademark use to refer to the entire line using the plural form. A noun may be singular or plural, but a trademark, which is a proper adjective, should be displayed only in the form in which it is established.

Correct use	Incorrect use
Nikon cameras	Nikons
Hamilton watches	Hamiltons
Parker pens	Parkers
Xerox copiers	Xeroxes

This rule is difficult to police, particularly for well-known products offered in a variety of styles or sizes. A recent news story appeared with the statement "Johnson & Johnson, the folks who bring you Band-Aids and other health care products . . . ." The trademark is Band-Aid, and the folks at Johnson & Johnson go to great lengths to make this clearly understood. To see one of their methods, the next time you apply a Band-Aid adhesive strip to a cut or scratched knee, notice the paper backing on the strip. The statement "Band-Aid is a trademark" is repeated over the entire surface. This not only presents the proper form of the mark, but also stresses the fact that Band-Aid identifies a particular origin and quality of adhesive strip.

In sales meetings or in in-house memos or correspondence, it is easy to slip into the jargon of plural trademarks: Varsols instead of Varsol solvents, Hoovers instead of Hoover vacuum cleaners, Kodaks instead of Kodak cameras, Thermopanes instead of Thermopane insulating glass and so on. It is bad trademark practice, as it is using the trademark generically.

Rule 5. Do not use a trademark as a possessive or as a verb.

Such use is generic use. A trademark cannot own anything. An advertising claim or package statement such as "ZAM's outstanding shine . . ." is improper generic use of the trademark. Moreover, a trademark is incapable of action; thus using it as a verb is also improper generic use (e.g., "When you ZAM your car . . ." or ". . . the satisfaction of ZAMMING your car . . ."). These statements can be turned around to mean the same thing while using the trademark properly: "The outstanding shine and protection obtained with ZAM car polish . . . ," "When you apply ZAM car polish . . . ," ". . . the satisfaction of a job well done following application of ZAM car polish . . . ," or similar wording. True, it may be necessary to use a few more words, but this challenges creativity.

LEVI'S, by the way, is a trademark of Levi Strauss and Company registered in the possessive form.

Trade names—the names under which a company conducts business—often appear in the possessive, even though identical to a company trademark. "Texaco's research has shown . . . ," "Mobil's sponsorship of the program . . . ," "Avon's chairman stated . . . ," "Xerox's announcement followed . . ." are trade name uses as opposed to trademark uses, and the possessive form in this context (i.e., as a company name) is harmless to the status of the identical trademark. Trade name use as exemplified here is in the informal style. The formal and legal trade name as used on documents, contracts, stock certificates, licenses, etc., would be the full company title.

Rule 6. Display the form of the trademark consistently.

Some trademarks include punctuation or consist of segments treated in a particular way. Be consistent in displaying the form of the trademark.

Marks made up of segments or including punctuation or both, which always appear consistently—at least when used by the owners—include JELL-O, TRU-Test, Gaines·burgers, MicroClassic, Close-up, Stir 'n Frost, Mug-O-Lunch, Nestle', and Drāno, among many others. Only through misuse would we see Jello, TRUtest, Gaines Burgers, Microclassic, CloseUp, Stir-and-Frost, Mugolunch, Nestle, Drano, or other variations.

Occasionally, one sees a model or grade number tagged on to a trademark by means of punctuation: ZAM-#2 Car Polish or ZING/Model 44 Jack Hammer. The hyphen and slash could be construed as modifications of the trademarks with the grade or model numbers as part of the trademark. ZAM and ZING are the marks to be displayed distinctively, not the generic terms "#2 car polish" or "model 44 jackhammer."

Correct use	Incorrect use
Tro-Mar marine lubricants	TroMar, Tro-mar
or	*or*
TRO-MAR marine lubricants	TROmar

(Tro-Mar is a registered trademark of Exxon Corporation.)

Rule 7. Do not combine trademarks.

Exxon Company, U.S.A., manufactures various types of lubricants and markets them under individual brands, such as Uniflo motor oil, Fanox cutting fluids, Teresstic industrial oils, and many others. If the company were to publicize these products as Exxon Uniflo, Exxon Fanox, and Exxon Teresstic, it might be construed that others manufacture Uniflo motor oil, Fanox cutting fluids, and Teresstic industrial oils. When trademarks are combined, the second mark can be placed in jeopardy through the inference that it is the generic name of the product.

Additional Rules for Design Trademarks

Symbols or designs established as trademarks should be reproduced as faithfully and as accurately as possible. With today's equipment for graphic reproduction, there is little excuse for doing otherwise.

Rule 8. Reproduce the graphic form of the trademark precisely.

The original shape of the symbol will lose its distinctiveness if variations are allowed.

Our fictional ZAM Industries uses as a basic trademark this design:

ZAM Industries should not permit:

Tampering with a design established as a trademark should never be permitted, as variants of a design eventually destroy the unique character of the original. If, for example, the trademark is based on an oval having a specific ratio between the major and minor axes, always maintain that ratio. If flattening or fattening the oval were to be permitted, the original would become lost in a blur of ovals of various proportions, a possible source of confusion to customers, and a mark difficult to defend against imitation because no one proportion predominates.

Rule 9. If color is included, use the color consistently.

When color is part of the mark, as it is in a multitude of trademarks, it should be used consistently to maintain distinctiveness. Random color use, that is, nonconformity to the basic color pattern of the trademark, destroys distinctiveness and also could result in a pattern of color confusingly similar to some other colored trademark.

If a trademark owner permits indiscriminate use of color, thus allowing the mark to lose its distinctiveness, that owner may find it difficult to defend the basic color pattern against usurpers. For example, the ZAM symbol outline is green, the letters are red, and the background is yellow. The people at ZAM often interchanged the colors, making the outline red, the letters yellow, and the background green, and frequently used other color combinations such as brown, orange, and tan. They did this thinking it was a good way to distinguish data sheets for different types of products. The ZING Company adopted a trademark similar to ZAM's original green outline, red letters, and yellow background. ZAM found it difficult to defend its basic color pattern against ZING's use because ZAM permitted many variations, no one of which was consistently dominant.

Of course, a colored trademark will be reproduced in black and white in most newspapers, in many magazines, and on black and white TV sets, all of which is standard trademark practice. In some situations, however, it may be impractical to print a colored trademark either in its full colors or in black and white. Generally, no harm comes to a colored mark through infrequent appearances in color other than its official dress. In fact, such appearances may help ward off would-be usurpers imitating the basic design but using other colors. It should be understood, however, that major displays of a colored design trademark, such as on billboards, packages, or other prominent displays, and the majority of appearances in media advertising should be in all the official colors. The official colored version should be so firmly impressed on the public's mind (or should constitute the majority of displays on public view) that infrequent or occasional displays in some other color do not create confusion as to what the mark actually is. The use of random colors should be controlled carefully as special situations requiring special permission of the trademark administrator. It should never become an authorized regular practice.

Rule 10. Do not embellish or otherwise modify a graphic trademark.

To promote certain concepts for using its car polish, ZAM came up with these variations of its trademark:

In effect, ZAM created two new trademarks, to the detriment of the basic ZAM symbol. Variations of a symbol or graphic, if permitted, can cause the basic graphic to lose distinctiveness, and eventually the trademark may be out of control.

Rule 11. Do not use the graphic outline as a frame for messages or illustrations.

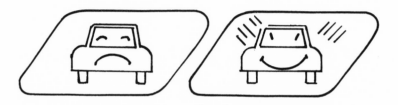

ZAM used these variations on its graphic trademark to promote the idea of a sad or happy car depending on whether it had been ZAMMED! Its basic trademark outline was thereby reduced to a frame or a background device, again detracting from its distinctiveness. And, of course, the idea of a car being ZAMMED is a direct violation of Rule 5.

Rules 8 through 12, concerning graphic trademarks, stress maintenance of graphic distinctiveness through maintenance of graphic purity. Variants in violation of these rules invite further tampering with the trademark and eventual loss of the distinctiveness that sets it apart from others. Many companies have on their staffs either self-taught or professionally trained artists who feel they can improve the company trademark, or who have a brilliant idea for decorating or modifying it for use in an unusual promotion or advertisement. The trademark manager should never give in to these adaptations. If indeed the mark becomes outmoded and needs improvement, then outside professional help should be sought, as discussed in Chapter 11.

Rule 12. Show trademark status.

The guidelines of Rule 3 for proper display of trademark status apply equally to graphic trademarks.

Rule 13. A company misusing its own trademarks cannot expect others to use them properly.

As a converse to this rule, treat someone else's trademark with the same respect with which you expect others to treat yours. The trademark owner must set the example.

Trademarks in Television and Radio Advertising

The rules and guidelines promulgated in this chapter should be applied so far as possible to television and radio advertising. Costly time is involved and pictures or words that take up valuable seconds must be trimmed to a minimum. This does not excuse, however, misuse or improper use of trademarks.

Several good trademark practices are used in TV commercials. Many include a display of the product packages and frequently a close-up of the package label. If the packages or labels display the trademarks properly and adequately, trademark protection is provided even though the statements may be too small to read on some TV screens. Some commercials conclude with a screen-filling display of the sponsor's symbol or graphic trademark, with the circled R or other form of registration notice plainly visible. Occasionally, one may see at the conclusion of a commercial, usually at the bottom of the screen and in small type, a flash statement such as "ZAM is a registered trademark."

Radio commercials are primarily a matter of maximum message in a minimum amount of time. Seldom is time available to explain, for example, that ZAM is a registered trademark of ZAM Industries. If time is available, so much the better, particularly when a new trademark is being introduced. In preparing commercials for radio, agencies should review and keep in mind especially Rules 2, 4, 5, and 7.

Your Trademark—A Common Household Word?

You may want your trademark to be well known in every household, but the last thing you should want is for it to become a *common* household word. Such was the fate of *aspirin, linoleum, escalator,* and *cellophane,* to name some of the more famous lost trademarks.

It is surprising the risks to which some owners expose their trademarks in advertising and sometimes on their packages, risks that detract from the mark's distinctiveness and erode its value. This need not be if the rules are followed and the marks are managed properly.

Trademark
Management Structures

Trademarks must be tended regularly and carefully, probably as much so as any other company asset. For this purpose, a company should have an established and recognized trademark management structure presiding over the selection and use of its marks. If it lacks such central control, the selection and use of its trademarks may get completely out of hand. Trademarks out of control may not only damage a company's image or the image of its products, but they also may become ineffective as marketing devices or may be lost entirely. Trademarks do not take care of themselves, nor can a company expect its employees to watch out for them without proper and adequate guidance.

The trademark administrative structure need not be complex. Nor is the establishment of a trademarks "empire" within any company suggested. The emphasis is provision for *central control of a company's trademarks as highly valuable business assets that grow in value and effectiveness when properly tended.*

It is recommended here that the central control—the trademark administration—be positioned outside the company's legal department, preferably within the marketing department since it is the primary user of trademarks. Focusing trademark administration outside the legal department can bring to the administration a variety of experiences and disciplines, and, when the department is properly backed by management, such placement emphasizes corporate concern for its trademarks. It is the contention here that the legal department, rather than being the central trademark administrative body, should be an integral part—a service arm—of the total administration. Attorneys generally are busy with a wide variety of corporate legal matters, and often are inaccessible when trademark problems, many of which could well be handled by authority outside the legal department, happen to arise.

The ideal trademark administrative structure depends on the size of the company and the number and diversity of trademarks to be controlled. The structure may consist of one person, a small group, or a committee headed by a top official of the company. The main point is that whatever the number of trademarks, top management should *establish a trademark administration and give it complete backing.*

As to time requirements, very few companies have trademark involvement large enough to justify a full-time trademark administrator or a full-time in-house trademark attorney. When a trademark administration is first established, one person might devote nearly full time to taking inventory, preparing statements of objectives and policies, and setting up rules and procedures. Once that is done, if done properly, the time requirement will drop to a relatively small fraction of one person's full time, assuming a company of modest size with a few trademarks. Large companies owning dozens or hundreds of marks and having extensive trademark involvement will have a staff of one or more full-time trademark attorneys and may have one or more nonattorneys working full time on trademark administration.

Much of the material in this chapter and the next is based on experiences within a large international corporation with diverse operations and interests. Not all the suggestions or recommendations are applicable or even suitable to every company owning trademarks, as the vast majority of such companies are relatively small and have relatively few trademarks to manage. The contents of this chapter and Chapter 9 are offered as a "menu" from which a company may select the items best suited to its particular needs and purposes. The overall functions and responsibilities of trademark administration are discussed in this chapter, followed by descriptions of possible management structures. Chapter 9 describes various basic documents and activities of trademark administration.

Basic Functions and Responsibilities of Trademark Administration

Whatever structure or system a company adopts, it should include provision for four aspects of trademark management: the final authority, the legal aspects, coordination of all trademark-related activities, and the keeping of records.

Final Authority

The final authority for important trademark decisions (other than strictly legal interpretations or actions) should be with top management—either the president or the marketing vice president or other top official directly involved in corporate management. If a committee is established for trademarks, it might be headed by the official having final authority, or by a person sufficiently high in management to have daily access to the president or other officer to whom final trademark authority is assigned.

The involvement of the person with final authority includes (1) approving the company's trademark objectives and policies; (2) approving proposed new trademarks; (3) approving trademark licensing agreements, either as the person having legal authority to sign such agreements on behalf of the company or as advisor to the officer whose signature is required; (4) approving trademark sales or purchases; and (5) advising counsel as to the extent of company involvement in legal matters with other companies over trademark rights or infringements. It is highly unlikely that the person with final authority would want to become involved in all trademark matters, nor in most instances should he want to, as many are sufficiently routine to be handled by lower-level personnel.

Legal Aspects

It is not the intent here to advise companies how to establish and operate a legal department for their trademarks. Legal department trademark activities listed below are intended simply to convey to others in trademark administration the activities that should be referred to, supervised by, or handled by trademark counsel:

(1) ordering trademark availability searches* and analyzing the results; (2) registering trademarks and maintaining registrations*; (3) preparing trademark licensing agreements; (4) negotiating trademark purchases or sales; (5) handling all matters of infringements or questions of trademark rights; (6) endorsing the company's trademark objectives, policies, and procedures or rules; (7) periodically reviewing company trademark uses for compliance with legal requirements; and (8) calling management's attention to significant changes in trademark or other laws that might affect the company's uses of its marks.

Small companies with no legal department but owning a modest trademark inventory would do well to retain outside counsel with solid trademark experience to handle its trademarks, in addition to whatever counsel it might retain for general corporate affairs.

Coordination

An important function of trademark administration is providing coordination, and a focus of responsibility, for the company's trademarks in all but strictly legal matters. This is the office to which questions, needs, or problems should be referred in the first instance, whether arising from inside or outside the company. It may be the office of the trademark "administrator," "coordinator," "manager," or "secretary of the trademark committee." Whatever title is assigned, it is recommended that the duties of this trademark administrator be assigned to someone other than an attorney. In small companies, in-house counsel probably would have a full range of legal responsibilities, with trademark matters occupying only as much of his or her time as absolutely essential. A nonattorney administrator would relieve in-house counsel of nonlegal chores involving trademarks. In large companies having a full-time trademark legal staff, an administrator from outside the legal department could bring to the trademark administration additional perspective and knowledge of the company, as well as handle many nonlegal trademark matters.

---

*An experienced nonattorney could in many instances handle adequately the routines of ordering searches and filing registration applications and renewals. Searches, however, should be referred to a trademark attorney for final analysis.

The administrator should have authority second to that of the final authority to act on various nonlegal trademark matters. He or she may resolve needs or problems of a routine nature without the necessity of involving higher-level executives or counsel. The administrator also keeps track of needs or problems that must be referred to others and expedites their completion. If trademark questions or problems are referred at random throughout a company (i.e., without central coordination), important needs or problems may fall into a crack and go unattended for weeks or months. Finally, the trademark administrator serves as liaison for trademark matters among the various company interests, particularly between the marketers and trademark counsel and between affiliates or branches and company headquarters.

Many trademark matters involving strictly legal considerations or technicalities should be referred in the first instance to trademark counsel. The administrator becomes involved in such matters only when legal involvement or action has bearing on the trademark activities of other departments of the company.

Record Keeping

Trademarks grow in value with age. Files should be established for every trademark when first considered and kept as part of the company's permanent records. Even if a mark is discontinued, its records should remain on file in the event it is decided to reestablish use, sell the mark, or take action against imitative use by others.

A separate file for each mark should include records of availability searches, evidence of first use, registration certificates, license agreements if any, and all other correspondence and documents relating to the mark. The total record for any particular mark could prove invaluable if rights to the mark are ever challenged in or out of court. Also, if it is decided to sell the mark, the record provides a basis for establishing its price.

Because most matters of record involve legal considerations or actions, trademark files usually are maintained by and within the legal department.

The record system should include a summary slate of registration renewals or other maintenance actions necessary for the ensuing year. The slate should be reviewed by the trademark administrator or the trademark committee well in advance of the action dates to determine whether the renewal or other action is to be completed.

A company with a large inventory of trademarks and registrations might consider using a computer to record and retrieve the essential data for each of its marks. Exxon Corporation, for example, has the worldwide registration, licensing, and other pertinent data for many hundreds of company-owned trademarks, involving thousands of registrations, entered in a computer system they call TIGERS (Trademark Information Gathering, Evaluation and Retrieval System). Through TIGERS, Exxon trademark attorneys and administrators can obtain almost any combination of information needed for trademark maintenance. Among other advantages, TIGERS provides the data needed for the annual maintenance review, replacing the arduous task of hand-sorting individual summary cards or searching separate files and preparing the maintenance slate.

The activities of these four separate branches—final authority, legal aspects, coordination, and record keeping—should be unified by means of either a formal or informal structure. A trademark administration or committee will provide unified action on trademark matters. It ensures that all matters needing attention are properly channeled and appropriate actions are taken. Further, it provides the watchdog for all the company's trademark assets.

Management Structures

Committee Systems

As with almost every organization and its activities, the committee system of trademark management has many advantages and certain disadvantages.

A committee can bring to trademark management a variety of disciplines, experiences, and perspectives, and can provide greater assurance that all company interests are considered in the process. Varied representation on the committee including members from different departments of the company, different product lines, and foreign as well as domestic interests also helps spread awareness of and concern for trademarks through several company activities. A major difficulty of most committees is the frequent postponement or disruption of regular meetings or attendance by the pressures of other work of greater immediacy. Also, trademark committees suffer the problem common to all committees: the occasional lack of unanimity that results in the creation of a camel when the objective was to create a horse.

In addition to a carefully prepared agenda for each regular meeting, a docket of items for committee consideration at various times of the year helps assure proper attention to all the company's trademark assets and their manner of use. For example, every January the committee might review trademark use on company packaging; February, facility identification; March and October, a status review of important legal matters and actions; and so on. One of the late summer or early fall meetings should include a review of registration renewals needed during the coming year and decisions as to the actions to be taken.

A small committee might be chaired by the vice president for marketing or corporate affairs and include in-house counsel and a trademark administrator. The administrator could serve as the committee secretary. If the company does not have inside counsel, the post might best be filled by the person who would have most frequent contact with outside counsel.

A company offering a diversity of products could do well with a larger committee having representation from each of its different product branches, plus members representing the overall or corporate interests, together with legal representation. The broader the representation, the less likely it is that one division or entity will work in conflict with another or in conflict with company trademark policies and procedures.

An example of the committee system is that of a U.S.-based manufacturer of ethical pharmaceuticals and other products. The company operates internationally. Its trademark inventory is approximately 250, and the company establishes some six to eight new trademarks each year. The trademark committee consists of eight members headed by the administrator for new product activities, corporate business development. Other committee members include a company attorney for domestic affairs, a company attorney for international affairs, two representatives of domestic marketing, two from international marketing, and one from research and development. The committee meets regularly. It does not have full authority on all trademark matters, as final authority rests with the president of the company.

Noncommittee Structures

One-person, part-time management   Probably the most typical trademark management, at least within smaller companies or companies having only a limited number of trademarks, is that assigned to one person within the company as part of his or her overall responsibilities. Either the small management staff or the company's few trademarks warrant attention to trademarks only infrequently, usually as needs or problems arise.

For such situations, trademark administration is probably best assigned to a member of the marketing department or the executive staff. Whoever has the assignment must provide maximum service to company branches using the trademarks and work in close liaison with the company's legal department or outside counsel. This includes preparing and issuing guidelines for proper use of the company's marks, assisting in getting maximum benefit from those uses, and coordinating or assisting in the proper and adequate protection of the marks through registrations and vigilance for infringements.

The one-person, part-time administrator probably would not have final authority on trademark matters of major importance. More likely, the adoption of new marks and other "final authority" matters would be referred to one of the top officers of the company.

The part-time trademark administrator would be well advised to prepare and make maximum use of at least a policy statement, a statement of rules or procedures, and a style guide. (These documents are described in the next chapter.) None need be elaborate. For a small company, one document might cover all three. By distributing the document or documents to officials, departments, and secretaries throughout the company, the trademark administrator at least makes others aware of the company's concern for its trademark assets. Periodic reminders through in-house media also help. Employees cannot be expected to use trademarks properly unless they are informed. When a trademark-use infraction occurs within the company, it usually stems from ignorance of any authority, rules, or procedures rather than from disregard of them.

Another aid for the one-person, part-time trademark administrator is an annual or biennial meeting of staff members and heads of the departments using company trademarks. An hour's time devoted to explaining to them the fundamentals of trademarks and a review of company policy and procedures can pay dividends in improved awareness and cooperation.

One U.S.-based manufacturer of flat glass products manages its inventory of about fifty-five trademarks without a committee through an essentially one-person, part-time operation. The company establishes one or two new trademarks each year, and its operations extend into several foreign countries. Most of the company's trademark administrative duties are handled by a member of its in-house legal department. Responsibility and final authority rest with the vice president for corporate affairs, who is responsible also for developing new trademarks and trademark use. The company does not have a trademark style guide.

Another U.S.-based firm, of approximately the same size as the above, has rather varied but limited lines of products, including certain food commodities and machine tools. Its trademark inventory and needs are similar to those of the glass manufacturer, and it too functions without a committee. New marks are suggested by the business line manager and reviewed by a corporate attorney. The corporate attorney orders availability searches but turns to outside counsel for filing registrations and occasionally for advice on search reports. The firm publishes a detailed trademark style guide through the office of the corporate secretary. Questions regarding trademark use or adoption are referred first to the attorney responsible for trademarks, who may work with the head of the business line in problem resolution. Occasionally, difficult matters may be taken to the corporate general counsel, who has final authority for all trademark legal matters. Policy matters, which arise only rarely, may be handled by the general counsel or referred to the board of directors or to the president.

Full-time operations   The trademark involvement of most companies does not justify a full-time trademark administration, even by only one person. However, a description of the operations as carried out by two large companies having essentially full-time staffs for trademarks may be of interest, and may provide ideas for companies of intermediate sizes.

A large U.S. consumer-products company, operating in over 100 countries, is widely known as a manufacturer of quality cookies, crackers, snacks, and cereal products. It also has a line of pet foods and lines of nonfood products including toiletries, pharmaceutical products, and household accessories. The company owns between 250 and 300 trademarks protected by some 350 U.S. registrations and about 1,500 foreign registrations. New products require some fifteen to twenty-five new trademarks each year.

For new products within any particular product line, the brand manager is responsible for proposing candidate trademarks. The brand manager may work with an advertising agency in creating proposed marks. The list of proposed marks is turned over to the trademark group in the corporate legal department. (The group encourages short lists of carefully considered proposed marks, rather than lengthy lists of suggestions made at random with the hope that something will survive.) Within the trademark group, the marks are screened for conflicts by comparison with various published lists of existing marks, and reviewed to determine registerability. The trademark group boils the list down to perhaps two or three of the most promising marks and orders professional searches. Search results are analyzed within the group. Final choice of a new mark is up to the brand manager.

The trademark group consists of a trademark attorney and three nonattorney assistants. The routines, including ordering searches, preparing registration applications, renewing registrations, and maintaining records, as well as reviewing trademark use on packages and in advertising, are handled by the three nonattorneys. The group leader of the three has many years of broad experience within the company and is responsible to the trademark attorney as head of the trademark administration. The company does not publish a style guide.

The corporate managers of the various product divisions are responsible for liaison on trademark matters with the company's many affiliates and operating divisions. In most instances, the contact within the affiliate or operating division is the president of the affiliate or head of the division.

One of the largest international corporations uses a committeelike structure, without the formality of a committee organization, to control and manage its trademarks. The company's major interests are petroleum and petroleum products and petrochemicals. It also has interests in coal, nuclear fuel, new technology energy systems, information systems, and information systems equipment. Its trademark inventory is about 1,000. Affiliates of the company operate in every continent.

Overall responsibility for the corporation's trademarks, used by the affiliates worldwide, is placed with the vice president for petroleum products. He may refer trademark matters of major worldwide consequence to the management committee within the board of directors. Much authority for trademarks rests with the manager of the marketing operations division within the petroleum products department. In turn, a trademark administrator within marketing operations handles or coordinates many of the matters needing headquarters attention. Persons within the marketing operations division responsible for trademarks—including product branding, use on packages, identification, and advertising—work in close liaison with the four trademark attorneys in the corporation's legal department.

The petroleum operations of this corporation are divided into five international regions or operating organizations, each with its own headquarters. Each has a trademark coordinator, a responsibility assigned usually to the marketing head for the region or organization, to oversee trademark use and control throughout the region. The regional trademark coordinator works directly with the corporate trademark administrator, or may at his option refer problems directly to the head of marketing operations.

Within the five geographical regions, individual affiliates or divisions report to the headquarters for the region. These affiliates or divisions also have a trademark representative, usually a marketer, for contacts with the regional headquarters. The affiliates or divisions must refer their trademark questions or problems to their respective headquarters. They are not permitted to bypass their regional headquarters for direct reference of their trademark problems to corporate headquarters. Working under a set of guidelines issued by the corporate trademark administration, the regional headquarters coordinator has authority to resolve certain types of problems without referring them to corporate headquarters.

The corporation's trademark attorneys also have a worldwide network of counsel that includes in-house counsel for regional headquarters and larger affiliates, outside counsel serving the smaller affiliates, and outside firms specializing in trademarks in countries where such firms are established.

The persons in marketing operations involved in trademarks and the trademark attorneys, all at corporate headquarters, serve as a loosely formed administrative committee. The trademark administrator and his contacts at regional headquarters serve as a second-level structure, also without formal committee organization. Because of the diversity of problems and concerns, the informal committee structure provides more operational flexibility than is possible with a formal committee operating under rules of parliamentary procedure. At the same time, the network provides access to worldwide information and opinion when necessary.

Within the corporate structure, the trademark attorneys work closely with the marketers whenever any legal aspect of trademarks might be related to a marketing aspect. For example, the trademark attorneys and the trademark administrator annually review trademarks due for registration renewal during the coming year. The administrator advises the attorneys whether to renew each particular mark in each country, taking into consideration the current or potential interest or use of the mark in that country. Situations arise, of course, when additional information is needed, and the regional-affiliate structure outlined above is utilized to obtain it. The attorneys may see reasons that transcend marketing considerations for renewing a registration, and may—and frequently do—override a recommendation from the marketers to let the registration lapse.

A second example of marketing and legal cooperation involves the more complicated matters of infringements and sometimes trademark purchases and what particular course of action to follow. The corporate trademark attorneys meet periodically with the corporate marketing officials, including the trademark administrator, and review current problems, actions they are taking or propose to take, and probable costs involved. The marketers are able to provide additional information in many instances that helps keep the problem in perspective. Without such assistance from marketing, the attorneys have a somewhat limited basis upon which to judge further courses of action or the settlement value of any particular case. Of course, not all trademark conflicts or problems faced by the attorneys are referred to marketing. Many are relatively minor, involve little or no cost, and often can be resolved by a single letter or a telephone call by trademark counsel. Sometimes, too, a particular course of action for the attorneys is so clear-cut as to be independent of any information or opinion supplied by the marketers.

The petrochemicals branch of the company's business, having need for its own set of trademarks, operates in a manner similar to that described above, and almost autonomously. The operation has its own trademark administrator within its public affairs department. He works closely with the corporation's trademark administrator and with the corporation's trademark attorneys. The petrochemicals trademark operation is responsible to the corporation's trademark administration for the trademarks established for and used by it.

In summary, there is no "best" way to administer trademarks. What may be highly suitable for one company may be inadequate for another. It is the author's firm belief that centering the entire operation within a firm's legal department is a mistake. Legal aspects of trademark administration are but a part of the overall trademarks picture. Marketers and other major users of a company's trademarks, as well as members of the legal staff, should be involved in their selection and administration. The use of outside advertising agencies or outside legal counsel often is necessary, but the basic responsibility cannot be shunted to such outside firms. It must be lodged within the company and, I strongly recommend, at top levels of marketing management.

Trademark Administration

Working Documents for the Central Authority

A central trademark authority should prepare a set of working documents as the basis for its actions and decisions. These documents provide an equal footing for everyone involved in trademark management as needs or problems arise. Without such guidelines, because trademark matters may arise infrequently or unpredictably, actions and decisions could become aimless or at variance with one another. This often is reflected in trademark use that appears to be aimless or inadequately controlled. Reliance on memory for precedent policy or action usually proves most unreliable.

The recommended working documents are listed below:

- inventory of trademarks
- statement of objectives
- statement of policies
- list of procedures or rules
- style guide

Trademark Inventory

The purpose of an inventory is to provide the trademark administration a brief working reference to all the trademarks a company owns or has owned. It should include not only the currently active marks, but also old marks no longer used, abandoned or sold marks (questions regarding such marks do come up from time to time), as well as new marks under consideration. With each mark, include a word or two describing the product or service to which it applies, indicate whether the mark is registered, and define its current use status. The inventory is primarily a reminder reference and is not intended as a complete history of each of the listed marks.

It would seem a foregone conclusion that someone in a company would know the trademarks it owns. But with changing personnel, company reorganizations, expansions, or divestitures, and particularly with older, larger, and more diverse companies, it is surprising the trademarks that drop out of sight in the shuffle and are subsequently uncovered by an inventory. Most of a company's trademarks will show up in the records of its legal department, assuming the marks were registered or were involved in a legal transaction. Others may show up in old price lists or sales manuals or in advertising files; some may have appeared in the company's in-house periodicals or newspapers. The inventory, in addition to providing a handy reference list, helps determine the framework and extent of statements of objectives, policies, and procedures.

A Statement of Objectives

What does the company expect of its trademarks insofar as management is concerned, and as seen by the public? A set of objectives might include the following concepts. They are tied directly to the functions of trademarks discussed in Chapter 3.

> The trademarks will be established and maintained to enhance the value and benefit of the company's products and services as perceived by the consumer (a) by identifying uniquely its products, services and facilities as distinct from those of competition, and consistent with business objectives; and (b) by communicating the quality aspect of the products and services through regulated and consistent use and display of the marks and adherence to quality standards for the products and services they identify.

A Trademark Policy Statement

A policy statement provides the administrative direction for fulfilling the trademark objectives. It also supplies the authority or framework upon which rules and procedures are built. The policy should be stated in general terms, and should be as brief and clear-cut as possible. The policy concepts listed here assume a broad international trademark involvement. Not all apply to every company and its particular trademark situation.

1. Recognize the central body—officer, group, or committee—as having total authority for selection, use, maintenance, and control of the company's trademarks.

2. Describe the conditions under which a trademark may be used, particularly as related to the standards the product must meet before the mark may be applied.

3. Require all branches or affiliates that manufacture a product meeting company standards to use the applicable trademark. Do not permit the branches or affiliates to establish their own marks for local use, except as may be necessary (see item 4).

4. Recognize the possible existence of unique situations, especially in foreign countries, in which the use of a trademark other than the company's established mark may be necessary (e.g., a conflicting mark may exist or the established mark may have an unfortunate connotation in the local language).

5. Stress the use of trademarks only in the approved manner and prohibit embellishments, modifications, or applications to products or services other than as defined for the marks.

6. Protect the trademarks through registration and ownership in the name of the corporation or parent company, or in the name of the affiliated company in foreign countries requiring local ownership of the trademarks.

7. Define the position of the company with respect to (a) licensing the use of its trademarks by others and (b) use of its trademarks by others as endorsements.

Statement of Procedures or Rules

The procedures should define the manner in which trademark matters throughout the company are to be referred to the central trademark authority for action. They should state clearly that independent action by a department, group, or individual outside the authority is not condoned.

The amount of detail in the procedures and instructions depends on the complexity of the company and its trademark inventory. Whereas the procedures should provide for the most common and most frequent situations, it is virtually impossible to foresee every situation or problem that might arise. Any problem not covered by the procedures can best be handled as it arises, using common sense and good judgment.

Among the items to consider in setting up procedures and rules are the following:

1. Proposals for new trademarks: the basis for the need; anticipated date of product or service introduction; will various product grade or model numbers be involved and what system of designating these is proposed; what are the major competitive qualities and marks for similar goods or services; where or in what type of market will the mark be used; what new marks does the requestor propose for consideration; endorsement of the proposal by the requestor's management.

2. The use of an established company trademark for the first time by a branch or affiliate: submission of proof that the branch or affiliate meets the quality or performance standards for the product associated with the mark, or justification for deviations from the standards.

3. Requests from outside the company to use a company trademark: regardless of purpose, all should be referred to the central authority. A trademark licensing agreement may or may not be needed. Many such requests are for essentially noncommercial uses and appear to be innocuous, such as for an educational display or for promoting activities benefiting local sports groups, first-aid groups, or fire squadrons and the like. The central authority may know reasons to approve or deny the request. Furthermore, it is not good trademark management policy to permit company personnel in the field to act on the random, apparently innocent request. Similarly, if such requests are addressed to company headquarters, the advice or opinion of the branch or affiliate where the mark is to be displayed should be solicited before the request is approved or denied.

4. Requests from within the company to use company marks on promotional items, awards, clothing, or for other purposes not

directly related to the basic function of the mark. Although such uses are largely taken for granted, requests through channels are important as a part of trademark control and for assurance that the marks are properly displayed.

5. Provide for the central authority's regular review and approval of company trademark use in advertising, package graphics, and identification prior to use.

Whether the document incorporating these concepts is called "rules" or "procedures" is largely a matter of in-house diplomacy. "Rules" seems to connote "this is the company law," and is a rather harsher term than "procedures." The latter term should probably be used if various branches of the company enjoy substantial autonomy in their operations.

Style Guide

The style guide is a brief statement of the proper use of the company's trademarks and can be one of the most useful tools for trademark administration. It need not be elaborate, and for a first or "trial" edition it might be informal and distributed on a limited basis by means of photocopies for review and suggestions. Questions probably will arise that were not considered in preparing the guide, and revisions or additions will then be necessary. When all appears to be in good order, a more formal guide may be prepared, professionally printed using the official company colors, and widely distributed.

The guide is distributed to management and office personnel throughout the company, to advertising agencies, major distributors of company products, or any other groups, organizations, or companies that might have reason to use or mention the company's marks. It can also be sent in fulfillment of random requests for information about the company's trademarks. The style guide should be a part of the package accompanying trademark licensing agreements or approvals for nonlicensed uses of the mark. The guide provides a useful means to remind the innocent and sometimes not-so-innocent misuser of company marks that there is a proper and approved way to use the mark.

Many companies prepare and distribute a style guide. Walt Disney Productions has a guide of four brief pages plus a cover entitled "The DISNEYLAND Trademark." The guide states the five basic rules of proper use of DISNEYLAND, using Mickey Mouse to illustrate the rules: highlight the mark, use the mark as an adjective, avoid the possessive, never use the mark as a geographical location, and use the symbol ®. The pamphlet concludes with a statement to members of the organization advising "What You Can Do" to help maintain the protection of the DISNEY-LAND mark.

Levi Strauss & Co. has a somewhat more elaborate brochure, "Levi's® Trademarks." Not only does the booklet illustrate present-day trademarks of the company, but it includes some of historical interest. The seven sections of this twelve-page style guide are titled What They Are and How They Are Used; The Most Important Trademark is Levi's®; The Levi's® Housemark; Levi's® Other Important Word Trademarks; Levi's® Design Trademarks; Be Alert for Trademark Abuse; and Unsolicited Ideas.

Kraft, Inc.'s, booklet "Kraft Trademarks" includes a brief statement of trademark value and purpose, trademark history, and basic rules for proper use of its marks. It illustrates, in color, various marks used by the company and its divisions for the wide variety of foods and other products it offers, including the Kraft housemarks, Sealtest dairy products, Whipped margarine and cream cheese products, and the Breyers and leaf design trademark on premium ice cream, among other Kraft-owned marks. The booklet concludes with a short paragraph entitled "When in doubt, ask the experts."

These three style guides, selected at random, are representative of those prepared by many companies. Any company owning even one trademark and not having a style guide should seriously consider preparing one.

Published policies, rules or procedures, and a style guide distributed throughout a company save a great deal of in-house indecision or argument. People within a company who write or display the trademarks appreciate guidelines and rules to follow. They then know they are doing it properly. Without rules, displays and uses will vary greatly and the inconsistencies could be damaging to the mark. Furthermore, the documents demonstrate diligence in controlling trademarks and could be important evidence should it become necessary to prove diligence in court.

Other Administrative Activities and Responsibilities

Many administrative responsibilities and activities have been suggested or discussed in the earlier parts of this chapter. There are others that warrant mention and perhaps some elaboration:

- coordinate new trademark development
- review proposed advertising
- review proposed package graphics and identification
- assist in developing trademark license agreements
- publicize the trademark activity
- maintain reproduction artwork and color standards
- maintain vigilance and coordinate corrective action
- report to management and to the trademark administrative structure

Coordinate New Trademark Development

The development of all new trademarks for a company should be coordinated by the central trademark authority or administrator. This group or individual has the best perspective on the company's overall trademark policies and interests. Independent actions by various company branches can lead to conflicts of trademark interest within the company, and possibly can bring on legal problems from outside the company. Certainly, the branch or affiliate needing a new trademark should be consulted, and its ideas encouraged, but the central authority must maintain firm control.

Review Proposed Advertising

All proposed company advertising and promotional items that will display company trademarks should be reviewed for proper trademark use before release. This may be out of the question for a large company with many different types of business, geographically dispersed, and each advertising independently. If it is impossible to check every advertisement before it is released, at least arrange to spot check company ads from different branches or divisions.

The central trademark authority should make itself known to all advertising arms of the company and make them fully aware of their responsibilities in handling company trademarks. The trademark style guide should be distributed to every company department and to every agency likely to prepare company advertising. The review of company advertising should not be limited to product promotions. Departments other than marketing (e.g., company employment offices) also advertise and sometimes their ads expose company trademarks. The following statement appeared in an employment opportunity ad in the *New York Times*, placed there by a well-known pharmaceutical firm: "Some of our brand names are so famous they have the rare distinction of being commonly used in place of the generic product name . . ." !!! Included were examples of their brands having this "rare distinction." This is the type of statement that causes trademark attorneys to reach for the aspirin bottle. Never should a company boast of the genericness of its brands, or invite the public to use its marks in the generic sense.

It is perhaps unfortunate that some advertising agencies, in their zealous searches for original and eye-catching advertisements, play fast and loose with a client's trademarks. Unless caught in time they can place a trademark in jeopardy. The most serious violation of proper use is an attempt to make the trademark a common household word, risking loss of the trademark if consumers should think of it as the generic term for the product. To invite, in advertising, generic use of a trademark is to walk on the thinnest of ice, taking unnecessary risks with a highly valuable business asset. Yet it is often done. A late 1979 advertisement by a manufacturer of zippers displayed a page from a dictionary, with the trademark of the manufacturer substituted for the word *zipper*, and with the regular dictionary definition of the noun *zipper* following it. The heading of the advertisement included ". . . we might even replace the word 'zipper' in the dictionary." And if they do, what would they then use for a trademark?

Scripts for radio or TV advertising should not be immune to review for proper trademark use. Commercials often use trademarks generically, particularly as a verb—"You are doing your car a favor when you are Zamming it."

In reviewing advertising, package graphics, and identification applications (as discussed below), the trademark-use review committee should resist the temptation to offer criticism beyond the scope of the review authorization—for example, criticizing the story board for a proposed television commercial, the layout or theme of an advertisement for the newspapers, or the overall appearance of a package. Such matters should be left to the experts who are paid to do those jobs, and reviews should be limited to the display and proper context of the company's trademarks. Of course, if the entire framework in which the mark is displayed constitutes improper trademark use, rejection of the total should be mandatory.

Review Proposed Package Graphics and Applications to Corporate Identity

Just as with proposed advertising, proposed new package graphics or extensions of the identification system should be reviewed for proper trademark use before adoption. Improper trademark displays on packages or within the identification system usually are more costly or more difficult to correct, if not caught in time, than are such displays in advertisements appearing in local newspapers. A package displaying a trademark improperly or an improperly identified company vehicle, for example, may be on view indefinitely (unless recalled for correction), while the "on view" life of an ad is relatively short.

Assist in Developing Trademark License Agreements

There are several types of licensing agreements involving the use of a company's trademarks. Any such agreement should be prepared, of course, by a qualified attorney. It is the intent here to discuss only certain aspects concerning the trademarks and the possible involvement of the administrator, as the details of licensing agreements are matters for counsel.

In considering and preparing a license agreement, it must be kept in mind that the trademark owner must control use of the trademark and its significance with respect to the origin and quality of the goods or services on which it is applied. The licensee must use the mark in the manner prescribed by the owner and only on the goods or services described in the license. Moreover, the owner should maintain the right to inspect at any time and on the licensee's property the goods or services involved, and to terminate the agreement if the product or service quality or trademark display is not according to specified standards. Misuse of a trademark by a licensee is equally as serious as misuse by the owner, as the owner is held responsible. No matter who is licensed to use the trademark, the mark points to its owner as the source of the goods or services and their quality.

Generally, a nonattorney trademark administrator is not involved in the preparation and execution of trademark licensing agreements. Counsel should keep the administrator informed, however. In a large and/or diverse company, the administrator may solicit or coordinate the gathering of information and opinions from various branches of the company regarding whether granting the license would create difficulties, or reasons for granting or denying the license.

Let us say, for example, a nationwide trucking firm receives a request to license its trademark to a toy manufacturer for display on a line of scale-model trucks to be sold at retail outlets nationwide. The trademark administrator for the trucking firm could notify the firm's major branch offices of the request and ask for any positive or negative reactions to it. Not only might this provide significant information, but it is also good trademark management diplomacy. Just as top management of a company should never be faced with trademark surprises, management personnel in the field should be kept informed of important trademark matters, and sometimes their opinions or knowledge of specific situations should be solicited. Often they can provide additional insight or pertinent information.

Publicize the Trademark Activity

Within most companies, the typical employee seldom or never needs trademark information in carrying out his or her duties. In fact, the majority of employees probably are unaware of the existence of a central trademark authority in companies where it is established. Therein lies a certain danger. Sooner or later someone, in ignorance or oversight, will create or foster a trademark blunder of no small consequence. To reduce the chances of such misfortune, it pays to publicize the company's trademark authority and its activities.

The trademark authority could make use of a house organ for publicity. Perhaps once every six months or once a year a paragraph or two or a feature story in the employees' weekly newspaper would remind readers of the importance of company trademarks and how they are managed. If the company telephone directory has its own classified section, "Trademark Administration" should be listed. The company's trademark style guide could well be included in the material handed to new employees of the office and to professional and managerial staffs.

An effective means of publicity within a company is a meeting or conference with the individuals and groups—including high-level management—directly involved with using company trademarks. Depending on the extent of personnel changes or organization within the company, such a meeting might be held every eighteen months or so. To put everyone in the meeting on an equal footing, start briefly with trademark basics—definitions and functions—followed by a review of company policies and procedures. Use visual aids. Limit the prepared part of the meeting to twenty or thirty minutes, then open the meeting for questions and discussions. A large company with geographically dispersed affiliates might schedule a biennial tour of its interests by members of its trademark control authority for reviews at the various localities. In every meeting of this nature, it is essential to have in attendance or as a speaker or discussion panel member a company attorney responsible for trademark legal matters. Questions invariably arise having legal aspects or implications, and the answers should be supplied by counsel.

Maintain Reproduction Artwork and Color Standards

Graphic displays of company trademarks should be controlled through professionally prepared reproduction artwork and color standards. First-quality printed copies of the reproduction art and chips or swatches of the color standards should be provided in fulfillment of all approved requests to reproduce the trademark. Never supply lesser quality art or copies clipped from advertisements or publications, as distortion creeps in, sharpness is lost, and colors drift. The trademark administrator should see that supplies of reproduction art and color standards are maintained and made available to all who need them.

Maintain Vigilance and Act to Correct Misuses

Despite published rules, publicity, and the best efforts of a trademark administrator or central authority, misuses and seemingly unauthorized uses of a company's trademarks will occur. To avoid damage to the marks, constant vigilance and corrective actions are necessary. A misuse or seemingly unauthorized use should be investigated as soon as it becomes apparent, and corrective steps taken when the situation is clear-cut. The longer misuses or unauthorized uses go uncorrected, the more difficult they become to correct. They frequently spawn others, and delay of corrective action may result in a trademark out of control.

Misuses may occur in printed news stories or ads, television news coverage, telephone or trade directories, dealers' displays of company products, at company sales meetings, or through any of the hundreds of other ways a trademark may be used or displayed. There is also the possibility of infringement of a company's trademark rights by another company whether inadvertent or fraudulent.*

All employees should be made aware of the need for vigilance and encouraged to call to the attention of the trademark administration any questionable uses or obvious misuses. *Employees themselves should not undertake corrective measures.* Trademark counsel is in the best position to determine the seriousness of a particular situation and any necessary action to be taken. All such matters must be referred to the central trademark authority (which

---

* Chapter 6 mentions publication in the *Official Gazette,* for opposition, trademarks that *appear* to be registerable. TCR Service, Inc., publishes a weekly list, *Trademark Alert®,* of *new trademark applications* filed with the U.S. Patent and Trademark Office. Publication in *Trademark Alert* is not a basis for filing opposition with the U.S. Patent and Trademark Office. It could serve as the basis for a trademark owner to contact the applicant about a mark that appears to be in conflict with the owned existing mark. For information regarding *Trademark Alert,* write to TCR Service, Inc., P.O. Box 936, Englewood Cliffs, N.J. 07632. Both the *Official Gazette* and *Trademark Alert* are suggested references for maintaining vigilance.

includes trademark counsel) for resolution or correction. An employee outside the trademark authority attempting personally to correct or solve the problem could create difficulties and possible expense for the company. Sometimes what appears to be unauthorized trademark use is indeed authorized use, and an on-the-spot confrontation could prove most embarrassing. On the other hand, an apparently unauthorized use of a trademark may be fraudulent use. Investigation and corrective action must be handled only by counsel. Taking the matter to court may well be necessary. Interference by an overzealous employee having no authority in the matter could be quite damaging.

Trademark misuse by the various news media is especially difficult to prevent or correct. Repeated or glaring errors by a particular newspaper or journal sometimes can be corrected by having counsel write a friendly letter to the editor, calling attention to proper use of the trademark. Several companies use national advertising to publicize the correct use of their trademarks. The Xerox Corporation is an example, among others.

According to McCarthy, there is no legal remedy for generic use of a trademark by the press. The appearance of a mark in the generic sense in books, magazines, and dictionaries is not absolute proof that the term is generic. The owner of the mark cannot be blamed for "negligence" by failing to sue to prevent generic use by the press, as there is no legal basis for doing so.[1]

In-house trademark infractions generally can be handled by the trademark administrator. A phone call or a friendly or humorous note to the offender usually corrects the situation.

The major burden of vigilance must be carried by members of the trademark administrative structure. It is impossible, of course, to cover everything. Misuses will occur that even the best vigilance cannot prevent. Even so, a watchful eye and corrective actions when the marks are misused are all important parts of trademark administration.

Report to Management and to the Trademark Administrative Structure

In a company with an established and effective trademark administrative structure, the trademark administration is relatively free of crisis, trauma, or panic-button activity. It is important, however, to keep management informed of developments or potential troubles that might require action by company officials. The question "Why wasn't I told about this before it reached this stage?" asked by the chief executive officer could be most embarrassing.

Earlier paragraphs have suggested keeping management informed of new trademark selection, licensing agreements, and trademark sales or purchases. The status of any trademark conflicts with other companies should be reviewed periodically with management, since frequently management must decide the extent to which the matter should be pursued, and just how much of the company's money should be spent in resolving the problem.

Periodic reports to management—either quarterly, semiannually, or annually, depending on the extent of trademark involvement—should be part of the responsibility of trademark administration. The trademark administrator should of course report any seemingly crucial matters to top management as they arise, rather than delay until the scheduled report.

If a trademark administrative structure is widespread, as it might be for a large company, the trademark administrator could make good use of a newsletter to members of the administration. Not only does this serve as a periodic reminder of their trademark responsibilities, but the newsletter also can be used to keep members informed of important or potentially important trademark developments both within and outside the company.

An Assortment of Situations and Problems

The types of situations or problems that a trademark administration may confront are as varied as the trademarks themselves. Some will be as important to the marketing arm as to the legal. Resolution usually requires the consideration and cooperation of both.

In certain instances of misuse or unauthorized use of a company's trademarks, there are limits beyond which corrective action may be impractical, or may stir up such notice as to blow the entire matter out of proportion. For example, to go after the local

first-aid squad's unpermitted play on your trademark in a fund rais-
ing campaign may bring more unfavorable publicity than you care
to have. It might be better to look the other way. The misuse is
temporary, local, and probably soon forgotten. After the deed, you
might send the squad a polite note thanking them for their community service (contribution enclosed) and suggesting they check
with you next time if they intend to make further display of your
mark.

A play on a trademark that would appear innocent enough to
those unfamiliar with trademark law could be an entirely different
matter if given broad exposure. In the fall of 1977, the deluge of
Christmas catalogs included one from a prestigious gift firm in
Texas. Among its offerings of Christmas cards was a plastic replica
in size, shape, and color of the Exxon credit card. The word
XXMAS, copying the interlocked X's of the Exxon design, replaced
EXXON.

Not only is the word EXXON a registered trademark, but also
registered are the unique form of the X's and the graphic design
of the Exxon sign, of which the Exxon credit card is a replica.
Following the dictates of trademark control required by law,
Exxon trademark attorneys pointed out to the gift house managers
the violation of Exxon's trademark rights and asked withdrawal of
the Christmas card from the gift offerings. The gift firm complied,
with apologies.

The press heard of the incident and had a field day. Editorials
appeared in nationally circulated newspapers with Exxon made out
as Scrooge, the big corporation pitting its weight against the little
fellow. Unfortunately, many editors and columnists are unaware of
trademark rights and the need to protect them, or even of proper
trademark use. Exxon did what it had to do. Big or little, a company must protect its trademark rights even at the risk of unfavorable publicity.

Practically all general literature on trademarks cites the loss of famous trademarks because they became generic, and mention of
such loss is made frequently throughout this text. How did these
losses occur?

In general, a trademark may be ruled generic because the
owner either encouraged its use as a common household word or

failed to take steps to prevent it from becoming a common household word. The public accepted the mark as the word describing all such products (i.e., as a generic term), rather than as the identity of a specific product from a specific source.

One of the most famous lost trademarks is Aspirin. Bayer lost Aspirin (at least in the United States) because the company tacitly invited the public to think of aspirin as a generic term. Early promotion of Bayer Aspirin failed to establish a generic term for the product, and Bayer was not about to ask the public to swallow the chemical name—acetyl salicylic acid—as the generic. The public didn't know what else to call the pills, and Aspirin became a common household word. Someone has suggested that if Bayer had taken the trouble to display "headache tablets" after the word "Aspirin," it might still have the trademark.

"Escalator" became the common public word for "moving stairway" and was lost as a trademark in much the same manner as aspirin. The original owners of the "Thermos" trademark for vacuum bottles encouraged public acceptance of "thermos" as a generic term. Early advertising (circa 1910) attempted to popularize "thermos bottle." A company catalog of the era stated "Thermos is a household word." Later, other makers of vacuum bottles challenged the trademark, claiming "thermos" had indeed become generic. The American Thermos Products Company attempted to recoup the word from the public domain through advertising and notice to the press when the word "thermos" rather than "Thermos" appeared. The courts ruled, however, that the attempts had come too late. The damage was done, and "thermos" became generic.

Du Pont lost "cellophane" because it used the word to describe the material, rather than as the trademark for the material. An early Du Pont promotion might have read something like this: "Cellophane is a new Du Pont paperlike wrapping material, strong, moisture-proof, fully transparent . . ." rather than "Cellophane is a trademark of the Du Pont Company for a new paperlike wrapping material . . ." etc. In actual use, Du Pont created "cellophane" as a generic term.

The troubles of aspirin, thermos, and cellophane also plagued "yo-yo," the spinning top on a string. Donald Duncan, Inc., who introduced the toy in the United States, registered and used

Yo-Yo as a trademark, but also used yo-yo as a generic term. Duncan's attempts to establish "return top" as the generic term for "Yo-Yo" were never publicly accepted. The slogan "If It Isn't a Duncan, It Isn't a Yo-Yo" appeared in advertising, using Yo-Yo as a generic name for the product. When the Duncan company attempted to stop infringement of Yo-Yo, the damage had already been done. Moreover, the defendant in the infringement case testified that the toy was of Oriental origin and that *yo-yo* was a common Philippine term for the toy. According to the testimony, the yo-yo had been introduced in the Philippines long before Duncan introduced it in the United States. Since no one introducing a foreign article under its recognized foreign name can monopolize the article or the name, the court ruled that *yo-yo* could not be appropriated as a trademark even though when Duncan first introduced the product in the United States, *yo-yo* had no general significance in this country.

Contrary to some measure of popular belief, "nylon" was never a trademark. The Du Pont Company created the name and announced it as a generic term in 1938. However, Du Pont has registered "Nylon" as a trademark in some countries and has permitted its exclusive patent licensees to do so in others. The trademark registrations are for protective purposes only, to prevent others from obtaining "Nylon" trademark registrations that could be used to harass or exact tribute from Du Pont or its patent licensees or members of the trade using the material. "All of these registrations were secured with the clear understanding of the parties applying for them that they were for protective purposes only and were not to be asserted against any use of 'nylon' as a generic term for polyamide materials by anyone."[2]

A trademark battle common to many companies is counterfeit use of their marks. Companies of high prestige, especially in the clothing and jewelry businesses, seem to be particularly victimized. In 1980, the clothing industry estimated at $10,000,000 the value of the popular blue denim jeans bearing counterfeit trademarks of famous manufacturers.

Street-corner vendors are notorious for hawking watches or other jewelry items bearing famous but counterfeit labels at half the price of the genuine. Gullible purchasers discover the fakery when the watch or jewelry needs repair, usually within days or weeks of the purchase, and take it to the firm whose mark it bears.

Cartier, a prestigious silver and jewelry firm based in Paris, has been waging a trademark battle against a Mexican firm that uses the Cartier trademark to identify its outlets and its merchandise, and even copies Cartier's catalog. The Mexican company has some fourteen outlets in Mexico City and other Mexican locations. Cartier registered its name in Mexico about forty years ago, but the Mexican firm succeeded in getting the name registered in 1973 and opened "Cartier" stores. The Paris-based Cartier has won twenty-two cases of trademark infringement against the Mexican firm but the legal rulings have yet to be carried out because of delays in the Mexican court system. Consequently, Cartier has announced it will open its own branch in a suburb of Mexico City almost adjacent to the largest outlet of the Mexican chain. It will also open a wholesale outlet to supply genuine Cartier merchandise to selected jewelry establishments. All this will be accompanied by widespread advertising and publicity.

An interesting case was reported by the press early in 1980. Johnny Carson is internationally known as an entertainer and is famous as host of TV's "Tonight Show." Viewers of this television offering are quite familiar with the introduction to his appearance on camera—"Here's Johnny." To millions of viewers, those two words mean but one thing: Johnny Carson. However, a manufacturer of portable outdoor toilets felt the phrase was too good to pass up as a trademark for his wares, and applied for trademark registration for "Here's Johnny" to identify these sanitary facilities. Mr. Carson objected, and the case came before a federal judge in Canada. The judge was told that 63 percent of those polled in a random survey had associated "Here's Johnny" with the television talk show. The judge accepted these findings, and ruled that "Here's Johnny" could not be registered as a trademark without Mr. Carson's permission.

Trademark registration cannot, of course, prevent usurpation and counterfeit use of a mark. However, in most countries it does provide a much more solid footing for legal counteraction.

Perhaps the largest and most extensive trade name and trademark change ever undertaken was that by Standard Oil Company (New Jersey) to Exxon Corporation and Exxon brands for its major products early in the 1970s.

It all began in 1906, when the federal government brought
suit against John D. Rockefeller's Standard Oil Trust under the
Sherman Antitrust Act. In 1911, the Supreme Court ruled for the
government, and the trust was broken up into thirty-four competing companies. Seven were allowed to continue use of the Standard Oil name. Each was restricted to an area of the United States
in its marketing activities and could not use the name "Standard
Oil" in the territory of any other Standard Oil.

The area for Standard Oil Company (New Jersey) was primarily the eastern coast of the United States. In 1923, "Jersey"
adopted the trademark ESSO for a wide variety of its products and
to identify its service stations. In the 1930s, Jersey entered the
service station business in the Midwest under the Esso name.
Standard Oil of Indiana challenged the use of ESSO, claiming it
was derived from "S.O.," meaning Standard Oil, and that Indiana
Standard had exclusive rights to the Standard Oil name in the
Middle West. The courts agreed, and Jersey was enjoined from
use of ESSO outside its original territory.

Jersey grew during these decades. Its major domestic affiliate
was Humble Oil and Refining Company, based in Houston. Its
chemical arm was Enjay Chemical Company. Its research organization was at first Standard Oil Development Company, a name
later changed to Esso Research and Engineering Company. Because of the trade name and trademark restrictions imposed by the
courts, Jersey marketers in forty-seven states were offering products as Esso in the eastern United States, as Humble in a few
Midwest states, and as Enco in parts of the Midwest and Far
West. Chemicals were identified as Enjay. Investors held stock
certificates for Standard Oil Company (New Jersey). Many consumers considered all Standard Oil companies as one, or at least
closely related. Sometimes, too, the press even attributed certain
activities to a particular Standard Oil company when in reality, it
wasn't *that* Standard Oil, but another.

The situation, as stated by an official of Humble, was a marketer's nightmare. Every product sold across the country had to
be packaged three ways: as Esso, as Enco, and as Humble. Credit
cards had to be applicable to the marketing areas, as did every
product data sheet, every advertisement, and every promotional
piece. Sponsorship of nationally televised programs had to be mon-

itored carefully, as separate versions of the commercials had to be aired in respective Esso, Enco, or Humble areas. Extreme care had to be taken that a case of Essolube Motor Oil was not shipped to an Enco territory in place of Encolube Motor Oil.

Some thought was given to changing everything across the nation to Enco, but many did not consider the name particularly outstanding or unique. Moreover, Esso was well established and much more valuable than Enco in the areas where Esso was permitted. It was obvious, however, that one name was needed for the corporation and for its United States affiliated companies.

The details and mechanics of the name change were well documented by the press at the time and continue to be subjects for special reports. (See for example the 1973 article by John Brooks and the 1978 study by Ben Enis, as listed in the Bibliography.) Standard Oil Company (New Jersey) became Exxon Corporation; Humble Oil and Refining Company became Exxon Company, U.S.A.; the "Esso" in Esso Research and Engineering Company, Esso International, and Esso Chemical Company, among others, was changed to "Exxon." Enjay Chemical Company—the domestic branch of the chemicals business—became Exxon Chemical Company U.S.A. Jersey Enterprises became Exxon Enterprises. Through the chemicals business and certain other companies, the Exxon trademark is in use in most countries of the world. However, outside the United States, petroleum marketing continues to be identified primarily as Esso and to sell Esso products.

Trademark Use by Others—from Manufacturer to Ultimate Customer

A branded product may pass through many hands between the time it leaves the manufacturer and the time it reaches the ultimate purchaser. Somewhere along the line, in the complexity of brokers, wholesalers, distributors, and retailers, trademarks of the product manufacturer will be used in promotions, in informational brochures or catalogs, on signs at distributor or dealer establishments, in trade and telephone directories, and so on.

The manufacturer/trademark owner, having branded the product according to rules for proper trademark use, has a further

a

REG. U.S. PAT. OFF.

b

obligation to ensure proper use of the trademark by subsequent
handlers and advertisers of the product. The best method is by
example. Of course, it is impossible for a trademark owner to police every use of a mark by every dealer handling or advertising
the product. The owner can, however, supply basic art and proto-
type layouts for merchandising or promotional displays, or at least
supply to possible users a simple, one-page style guide describing
the proper display of the trademark.

c

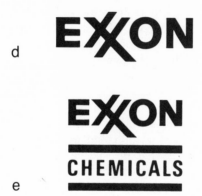

d

e

a. Standard Oil Company (New Jersey) trademark, circa 1925; **b.** the Esso trademark as used primarily outside the United States; **c.** the Exxon trademark used to identify service stations and petroleum products; **d.** the Exxon "logo" and **e.** the trademark of Exxon Chemical Company.

Discontinued Use of Trademarks

A manufacturer might discontinue a line of branded products but still wish to keep the trademark either for possible future use on other goods or to prevent someone else from using it. In the United States, failure to use a trademark for two consecutive years is considered abandonment. If the mark is to be preserved, it must be used. Occasional sales of products bearing the mark can be used as the basis for a truthful statement to a would-be usurper that the mark is in use. The courts, however, do not recognize as valid sales made solely to protect the trademark. If protection is desired, the mark must be put back into regular use as soon as possible as a primary brand.

Most trademarks that have been discontinued have served their day and might well be relegated to the wastebasket. Some marks become obsolete because the products they identify are obsolete. Others are no longer useful because of product failure resulting from poor quality, poor performance, or simply poor merchandising. Preserving obsolete marks can be more costly than they are worth. Before abandoning a mark, however, the owner should always consider, "Would I object, or would it harm my business, if someone else adopted this mark and used it on any type of product, including a product similar to that on which I used it?" If the answer is yes, then the owner must take steps to preserve the discontinued mark.

Somewhat akin to the problem of the discontinued product mark is that of selling or abandoning outlets identified by the company trademark. All traces of the company trademark should be removed from the abandoned or sold property. Otherwise, it might be occupied by someone who finds it easier or cheaper simply to modify existing signs by inserting his or her name. This can be a source of customer confusion because the basic appearance of the sign remains unchanged and many who see the sign will assume the original merchant is still in business on the premises. This can be deleterious to the original trademark. The same consideration applies to highway signs that a company discontinues.

There are notable exceptions to the perpetual obsolescence of retired trademarks. In 1968, RCA announced the retirement of Nipper, a black and white dog with his head in the horn of an old Victrola listening to "His Master's Voice." Nipper first appeared as a painting in 1890 by an English artist, Francis Barraus. The attentive canine first entered trademark service in 1901, when the Victor Talking Machine Company acquired rights to the picture. When RCA acquired the Victor company in 1929, the picture was used extensively in advertising, on labels of phonograph records, on phonographs and radios, and later on television sets. In 1968,

Nipper was retired when RCA modernized its corporate identity. Then, early in 1979, RCA announced the return of Nipper from retirement as part of a corporate program to make greater use of the dog and phonograph trademark.

10

Foreign Considerations

This chapter highlights some of the more important considerations for marketers in establishing and using trademarks outside the United States. Because of the many laws and their varying requirements, the discussion must of necessity be general.

Trademark laws around the world agree in principle to the concept and definition of a trademark—it must be distinctive or uncommon, it may not be descriptive of the quality, character, or function of the product, and it certainly may not be the common descriptive name or generic name of the product. All trademark laws provide for registration and renewal, although the laws differ in detail as to what is registerable. Outside the United States, trademark ownership is established by registration of the mark in civil law (statute law) countries, and by use of the mark in British law (common law) countries. In the latter, registration is based on use of the trademark or *intent* to use it. A majority of countries require "normal commercial use" to support registration, a requirement that is becoming more nearly universal as countries revise their trademark laws.

A commonality of trademark law stems from the International Convention for the Protection of Industrial Property of 1883, generally called the Paris Convention. This convention established reciprocity for trademark rights. Foreign owners of a trademark registered in a convention member country can obtain the same protection for their trademarks as in their home country. The convention also established protection of well-known trade names without registration, whether or not the trade name is part of a trademark. The International Classification System for goods and services (Chapter 6) was created by the convention, of which the United States is a member.

Registrations Outside the United States

The laws vary from country to country as to what is registerable as a trademark. In some countries, surnames are not registerable. In others, surnames can be registered if they have become distinctive (i.e., if they have achieved notoriety). Some countries do not register initials or numbers. The same considerations apply to geographical names. PHILADELPHIA, registered in the United States as a mark for cream cheese, is not necessarily registerable in other countries. The test or requirement is distinctiveness. Generally, civil law countries are more lenient as to what can be registered than are British law countries.

Registration of a trademark or common law ownership in the United States provides no protection for the mark elsewhere. However, a U.S. registration may serve as the basis for obtaining a registration in some countries. In civil law (statute law) countries, registration of a trademark is required to establish ownership and trademark rights. In the Commonwealth, or so-called British law (common law) countries, a claim to ownership may be established through use, as in the United States. Registration of a trademark in the common law countries is based on use of the trademark, or on intent to use it. (Intent to use a trademark is *not* a basis for registration in the United States.) Trademark registration in all countries provides a legal basis for defending the mark, so marks should be registered in every country where they are used or are expected to be used. Foreign registrations should be undertaken as early as possible, and well before marketing of the product, where trademark use is not a requirement for registration.

Foreign registrations should be considered when a new trademark is introduced in the United States. Even though present plans to market the new product are modest and limited to the United States, it is generally wise to protect the trademark in foreign markets as well. The new product may become more popular than expected, so that markets outside the United States can become important. If foreign trademark registrations are delayed until the product is introduced in foreign markets, it may be too late for their protection. Trademark pirates are on the lookout for good marks inadequately protected because foreign registrations are lacking. These predators register others' trademarks as their own in one or more countries, hoping to realize a substantial ransom when the originator of the mark attempts to register and use it. Whether a conflicting foreign registration is pure coincidence or the work of a pirate, there is little recourse other than to buy the conflicting mark or to apply a different trademark in the country where the conflict occurs. Of course, a trademark attorney in that country should be consulted to determine whether other remedies might be available.

Availability searches in foreign countries prior to registration are much more laborious than in the United States, since there are many countries to cover if broad geographical protection is sought, and few of these countries have professional searching services such as are available in the United States.

There are two possible ways to determine trademark availability in a foreign country. The first and probably faster method is to file for registration in the countries of interest. The applications will be rejected, of course, where conflicting registrations exist, and frequently the conflicting marks are cited. The second method is to retain a trademark attorney in the foreign country to search in the national trademark office for registered marks that might conflict with the mark of interest. Either method takes time.

It would be impractical in most instances to attempt searches in every country where the mark is to be used or may be used in the future. In Europe, searches at the International Bureau in Switzerland (see "International Registrations," below), in Great Britain, possibly in one of the Scandinavian countries, and in Japan, using the services of trademark attorneys in those countries, should indicate possible conflicts. In South America, searches in Brazil, Argentina, and possibly Colombia should be sufficient. Filing for registration is recommended over attempting a search in South America, because search organizations generally are nonexistent and governments will cite conflicting marks where they are registered.

A company in the United States may be interested in trademark protection overseas on a wide geographical basis but may not want the expense of it all at one time. Jerome Gilson, in *Trademark Protection and Practice,* offers a priority system to spread foreign registrations over a few years.[1] Initially and before a trademark is put into use in the United States, Gilson recommends filing in Canada, Mexico, Great Britain, and Japan. He then lists five additional groups of foreign countries for staged registration, based on marketing in the United States and expansion into foreign markets.

Filing for registration in some countries can be tedious and even onerous. Requirements differ as to the information to be supplied and the forms to be submitted. Issuance of registrations can be extremely slow. Although some countries may issue registrations within a year or two, five or six years is not uncommon. As to use and protection of a trademark between the date of filing and issuance of the registration, a trademark attorney in the country of interest should be consulted.

International Registrations under the Madrid Arrangement

For most countries, registrations must be filed with the individual governments, but there are some significant exceptions. An arrangement among some twenty mostly European countries,* in force since 1891, provides simultaneous filing of a trademark among these members. The arrangement is available only to nationals of the participating countries. The United States is not a member, nor is Great Britain.

To obtain an "international" registration through the International Bureau in Switzerland, the mark must first be registered in

---

*Algeria, Austria, Benelux (Belgium, the Netherlands, Luxembourg), Czechoslovakia, Egypt, France, East Germany, West Germany, Hungary, Italy, Liechtenstein, Monaco, Morocco, Portugal, Republic of Vietnam, Rumania, San Marino, Spain, Switzerland, Tunisia, Yugoslavia. The Soviet Union joined the Madrid arrangement in 1976.

a member or "home" country. The owner of the home country registration may then request his or her national trademark office to file for registration with the International Bureau. Upon filing, the International Bureau publishes the registration and communicates it to all its members. Each member country has a year in which to deny local registration. Otherwise, the international registration has the same effect as national registrations under the laws of the individual member countries.

An advantage of this system is that a trademark owner has but two filings (the home country and the international) to accomplish many. Moreover, it provides a simultaneous filing date in all member countries, and filing date can be important in controversies of ownership.

Since the United States is not a member of the Madrid arrangement, a company based in the United States cannot obtain an international registration. However, if the company has an affiliate in a Madrid arrangement country, the affiliate can file in its home country and follow with international registration.

In some respects, it is perhaps unfortunate that registrations under the Madrid arrangement have become known as "international" registrations. It is often necessary to explain to persons interested in foreign trademark protection but unfamiliar with the arrangement that "international" is not the same as "worldwide."

Benelux Registrations

Belgium, the Netherlands, and Luxembourg have a single registration, filed in The Hague, applying to all three countries. The trademark must be used commercially within three years after registration for continued protection. Use in one of the countries is valid use for all three.

African and Malagasy Union

Twelve African republics * provide a single registration among themselves. There is no national registration available within these countries individually.

*Benin (Dahomey), Cameroon, Central African Republic, Chad (Tchad), Gabon, Ivory Coast, Mauritania, Niger, People's Republic of Congo, Senegal, Togo, Upper Volta. The Malagasy Republic (Madagascar) withdrew at the end of 1976.

The Trademark Registration Treaty (TRT)

The United States has been a sponsor of a treaty designed to simplify international trademark registrations and protection. The treaty, signed at Vienna in 1973 by the United States and thirteen other countries, will be in force when ratified by five. It has been ratified by four countries as of 1980, but the United States has yet to ratify.

The basic intent of the TRT is to provide for all participating countries a single application, a single international registration, and a central record of trademark registrations. It is designed to overcome objections to certain provisions of the Madrid arrangement.[2]

The European Common Market Trademark

Work has been in progress since the 1960s to develop a "European" trademark system for the nations of the European Economic Community (EEC).* There is a great deal of commerce between the member nations, but no arrangement provides uniform registration for the trademarks involved. A company in a member nation doing business throughout the EEC must follow the dictates of trademark law not only in its home country, but also in the other member countries. However, details of these various trademark laws are sometimes at variance with one another, and some authorities think this inhibits trade under a single trademark. Creation of a Community trademark system would stimulate the trade of branded goods by simplifying registration and offering equivalent trademark protection.

Classes of Goods in Foreign Countries

As in the United States, a trademark is registered in foreign countries under specific classes of goods or services. Canada is an exception, having no classification system. The majority of countries use the International Classification (see Chapter 6). Those who do not use it have their own systems. The protection accorded

*Benelux (Belgium, the Netherlands, Luxembourg), Denmark, France, West Germany, Ireland, Italy, the United Kingdom.

within a class varies with the laws. In some countries, it is quite broad and in others extremely narrow.

Publication of Filing for Registration

Many countries publish official gazettes listing trademark applications for opposition, in a manner similar to publication in the *Official Gazette* in the United States. An international company interested in protecting its marks in foreign countries should examine these gazettes regularly for marks likely to conflict with the marks it owns.

Registration Notices

It is good practice to show trademark status as constructive public notice to trademark rights wherever the mark is used. Forms of registration notice, where they are required or provided for by a country's laws, vary as to text or display. Consequently, a company exporting branded products should determine the requirements or provisions for such notices in the importing country. Fraudulent display of a notice claiming local registration in countries where none exists can result in loss of the mark under the trademark laws of many governments. A few countries require the owner of a registered trademark to give public notice of the registration.

The circled R registration notice, ®, indicates trademark registration in the United States only and is meaningless as an indicator of foreign registrations. With possibly one or two exceptions, a symbol similar to it is not used elsewhere. A 1977 decree in Honduras makes mandatory the use of a "symbol R" or "Marca Registrada" with registered marks.

A company exporting branded products from the United States to a number of countries, using either its domestic U.S. package or an export package, could display a combination notice such as the following, assuming the trademarks are registered both in the United States and in several foreign countries:

Trademarks Reg. U.S. Pat. & Tm. Off.
Registered Trademarks
Marcas Registradas
Marques Déposeés

The combined notice may be too large for a small package or label, even in the smallest type, and a single notice such as "Registered Trademarks" or the local language equivalent might suffice. Again, check the trademark notice requirements of countries to which products are being exported.

Language Requirements

Very broadly, there are no specific language requirements for the display of a trademark. That is, the mark may be registered and used as established by the owner. An exception is the People's Republic of China, where trademark display in Chinese characters is required.

Language requirements for package labeling and product description may be another matter. Canada, for example, requires all package labels to be both in English and in French.

The "Normal Commercial Use" Requirement

The trademark laws of a majority of countries require local use of the mark to support the registration. Depending on the country, use must be established within one, two, three, or five years (or some other period) following registration, with three and five years being the most common. Failure to do so does not necessarily nullify the registration, but it does make the mark vulnerable to attack and possible takeover by others. In many countries, a trademark registration cannot be renewed if use of the mark has not been established.

Many of the laws specify "normal commercial use" without defining the term, and the term has not been tested in the courts. However, authorities generally agree that efforts to market and sell products displaying the trademark must be reasonable and genuine. The pattern of product success should be within the range of success for similar products in similar markets. There should be a reasonable pattern of growth, even though it be modest. Where "normal commercial use" is required, limited sales solely to protect the trademark might not be recognized as valid.

In the absence of definitive court decisions, it is possible only to raise questions as to what is "normal commercial use" satisfying the various trademark use requirements outside the United States. For example, a company's normal procedure might be to list its newly branded product in catalogs and price lists, prepare a product information sheet or brochure, advertise the product through selected popular media and trade publications, and await purchase orders. Does this satisfy the use requirements, or must the company sell annually 100 kilos, 1,000 kilos, or 100,000 kilos of the product? Authorities believe sales must follow product introduction for "commercial use" to be normal. If yearly sales of 100,000 kilos of a product are considered normal, will one sale of this quantity to one customer satisfy the requirements, or should it be closer to ten sales of 10,000 kilos each or 100 sales of 1,000 kilos each? How many customers must be involved? One can only sympathize with the court that ultimately must resolve these and similar considerations if the need to define "normal commercial use" reaches litigation.

Term of Registration and Costs

The duration of a trademark registration varies from country to country, as does the period for which the registration may be renewed. Very broadly, the time periods range between ten and twenty years, although other times are specified in some countries. Registration and renewal costs also vary widely.

Trademark Licensing

The trademark laws of various countries differ with respect to licensing. Generally speaking, laws of the majority make no specific reference to the permissibility or prohibition of licensing of trademarks, except in the British law countries, which specifically provide for licensing with what is called a Registered User entry. Some countries now do provide for the recording of a license.

Before World War II, in a large part of the world a license to use another's trademark was unlawful, or at least of doubtful validity, in that use by a licensee no longer distinguished the goods of the trademark owner and resulted in deception of the public.

Great Britain faced the problem of licensing (which had become an accepted fact in business life) by amending its law in 1938 to permit licensing through the Registered User procedure *provided* the licensor controlled the quality and nature of the goods. The United States provides for licensing in its 1946 act with its related company provision, which does not require any recording but *does* require that the licensor control the quality and nature of the product. The product must be the same after as before licensing. Uncontrolled licensing can cause the mark to lose its significance as a symbol of equal quality, and could be considered abandonment. In many civil law countries, although there is no statutory provision for licensing, court decisions have recognized its lawfulness under proper controls.

Foreign Affiliate Participation in Trademark Administration

The trademark administration of a company operating internationally should include representation by its affiliated companies in foreign countries. At least, it should provide direct and specific links with its foreign operations to attend to local trademark matters other than those attended to by attorneys. For many companies based in the United States, the legal aspects of trademarks in foreign countries are handled by outside trademark counsel retained in the specific countries. Unless specifically provided for in a trademark administrative structure, the marketing aspects of the trademarks used by the affiliates may be neglected entirely.

Within each foreign affiliate, a high-level marketer should be responsible for local trademark matters. This would be the person or office with whom the trademark administrator corresponds on trademark matters of concern to both the parent company and the local affiliate, and who also is responsible for local management—proper use and control—of the company's trademarks. Generally, it is not satisfactory simply to send the correspondence to the affiliate's marketing management, hoping the management will see fit to assign it for attention or action. A specific contact, operating within the affiliate and with responsibility as trademark manager, provides a higher degree of certainty for proper attention to the parent company's trademark assets.

The importance of a direct contact for the marketing aspects of trademarks is twofold. First, it underscores the parent company's concern for its trademarks. Second, it provides local coordination for nonlegal trademark matters, a focal point or "chain of command" through which local marketers and field or district offices obtain trademark instructions or to which they may bring trademark questions, and which in turn is responsible to the parent company's trademark administration. These matters should not be left to chance or to ad hoc contacts or to spur-of-the-moment procedures, hoping all will work out satisfactorily.

Here, for example, is how a question of trademark adoption might be handled by a foreign affiliate in the absence of specific marketing responsibility for trademarks. Someone in the foreign affiliate marketing department decides ZORK would be a good trademark for a new line of detergents, and the proposal to use ZORK goes to the affiliate marketing management. With the blessing of that management, the matter is referred to in-house counsel, who forwards it to outside trademark counsel. The latter finds no conflicting registration and reports to the client that, indeed, ZORK appears to be available as a trademark for detergents. The in-house attorney reports these findings to the marketers, and since ZORK thus has the approving nod of the affiliate legal department, the marketers adopt the mark and introduce ZORK in the local retail stores. Meanwhile, at the parent company's headquarters, the trademark administration is developing an internationally acceptable mark for the new detergents, unaware of the foreign affiliate's activity with ZORK. When the trademark administration adopts WHAM for the detergents, either the foreign affiliate must replace ZORK with WHAM—an operation that could be costly and difficult to explain to customers—or the parent company must accept ZORK as the local mark for its WHAM products. Conflicts such as these can be prevented for the most part if a local affiliate trademark coordinator or manager is established and recognized, and proper procedures are adopted and observed.

The job of trademark coordinator at the affiliate level occupies but a small fraction of one person's time, and usually only when problems arise. In the press of other business, the trademark responsibility generally receives low priority. It is up to the trademark administration at the parent headquarters to maintain awareness and interest through periodic reports or newsletters to the affiliate trademark coordinators and to include trademark matters as agenda items during direct visits.

11

The Trademark and Corporate Identity

A corporate image is what a company *seems* to be. Various segments of society perceive or imagine the company differently and attach different degrees of importance to it. It means one thing to customers, another to stockbrokers and shareholders, and still something else to competitors, governments, creditors, debtors, educators, students, employees, labor unions, neighbors, and other social groups or segments. The company image to some is favorable and to others unfavorable, and the success or failure of the company depends in large part on which of these views of it predominates.

An image is the composite of the intangible and tangible factors that form the basis for public and private judgment of the company. The intangible factors affecting a company's image include the attitude of the company within its community or neighborhood, public statements by company officials, its attitudes toward shareholders, its advertising methods and messages, the manner in which its employees react to customers, its political, social, and business customs, the manner in which it settles its debts, its aggressiveness, fairness, and evenhandedness, the services it provides, its courtesy and thoughtfulness, its credit and collection techniques, the way it solicits new business, its refund or replacement policies, its hiring and firing practices, its relationships with labor unions, its efforts and reputation in research and technology, company morale, and the environment and benefits it provides its workers.

Equally, there are hundreds of tangibles contributing to a company's image. Among them are the quality and price of its products or services, the material, shape, and convenience or utility of its products and product packages, the way its offices and plants are maintained, the measures it employs to prevent environmental pollution, and the location, cleanliness, and offerings of its retail outlets.

A crucial part of the tangible image is the corporate visual identity. *This is the orderly and consistent use and display of trademarks, designs, styles of type, and colors to communicate the company name, its places of business, the nature of the business, and its products and services.* However people perceive a particular visual identity, they are consciously or subconsciously forming opinions or images of the company responsible for it.

Corporate visual identity is composed of hundreds of elements. Included are business stationery and documents of every description; brochures and sales promotion material; annual reports, catalogs, point of purchase displays, posters, highway signs, vehicle identification, and product package graphics; the corporate trademark and product brand names; the marking or signs of retail outlets, factories, and offices; employee uniforms; the environmental designs of its facilities and reception areas; the manner in which the company is listed in telephone and trade directories; and countless specialized design applications. Every visible part of a corporation's facilities and physical assets contributes to company image and is within the scope of a corporate identification program.

A well-designed, well-implemented, and well-maintained corporate visual identification program can be a major business asset and a strong marketing tool.

Reasons for a Corporate Visual Identity Program

A corporate "visual identity program" is a continuous company activity that manages applications of the various elements constituting the coordinated visual identity scheme. Such administration is essential if the visual identity is to remain sharp and uncluttered. Without a central administration monitoring the program, the visual identity can rapidly become misapplied, distorted, and out of focus, no longer serving the objectives for which it was established. Administration of the visual identity could well go hand in hand with trademark administration, as discussed in previous chapters.

A part of administrative vigilance should be a watchful eye for the appropriate time for visual identity change, even to the extent of a major overhaul. Every company has a visual identity to some degree, whether planned or simply a consequence of being in business. Whatever the extent of the visual identity, is it the best that can be had? Does the identity reflect the type of company you wish the public to see? Is it ahead of or abreast of competition? Is it a memorable identity that attracts repeat business? Has the company diversified or expanded to such an extent that a new identity would better reflect its present nature and business?

Acquisitions, divestitures, major changes in product lines, new office buildings or new factories, changes in marketing methods or philosophies, the entry of new competitors with fresh appearances, changing social attitudes toward various types of identification, and even legal complications or restrictions involving your present identification are further reasons for considering a new corporate visual identity program.

The head of one large design firm stated that a corporation's visual identity should be reappraised and refurbished or replaced about every fifteen years. Beyond that, the identity begins to look outmoded.

A New Corporate Identity Program

Many companies have undertaken major new visual identity programs in the past decade or so. To name but a few, they include United Airlines, First National City Bank with its name change to Citibank, Radio Corporation of America when it changed to RCA, Standard Oil Company (New Jersey) when it became Exxon, the Bell System (A T & T), the Continental Group in its change from The Continental Can Company, and Gilbarco, which formerly was Gilbert and Barker. Even the Girl Scouts and the Boy Scouts recently refurbished their visual identities. All of these programs were the work of professional design firms.

New identities for two well-known organizations.

Initial Steps

The need for a new or refurbished identity often is first evident to top management, and frequently the idea to undertake an
identity program arises in the front office. A program undertaken
without management blessing and cooperation will at best be frag-
mented and more likely doomed to failure. The first step, then, is

to present for management's approval a proposal for a new program including an outline or summary of the steps and considerations recommended here.

Appoint an ad hoc committee. The purposes of the committee are to determine objectives for the program, select a professional design firm, assist the design firm when necessary, and receive and act upon the design firm's reports and recommendations. As work progresses, the central "steering" committee might well establish subcommittees to attend to various aspects of the program.

Bring together in the central committee representatives of top management, marketing, law, public affairs, engineering, advertising, and environmental concerns, along with others who have broad experience and knowledge of overall company policies and operations.

Seek professional help. Establishing a corporate visual identity and launching a new program is not a job for amateurs, however good their intentions may be. Perhaps the worst mistake a company can make in this area is to turn over to its drafting department the job of redesigning its trademark and other elements of its visual identity. Even though the draftsmen may be highly skilled in graphic arts, their point of view from within the company is too narrow. Moreover, they will face too many internal pressures and opinions. Experience, skill, and objective appraisal must be brought together in establishing an identity program, and this can best be done by a professional design firm.

Many fine design firms of vast experience and fine reputation are available worldwide. The names of these firms and examples of their work are in reference sources found in most well-stocked libraries. Comprehensive articles on corporate identification can often be found in journals such as *Art Direction, Advertising Age, Graphis, Industrial Design,* and sometimes *Fortune.*[1]

A classic reference in this field is Ben Rosen's book *The Corporate Search for Visual Identity.*[2] Rosen's work is a study of fifteen outstanding corporate design programs including those by Eastern Airlines, IBM, Mobil Oil Corporation, RCA, Olivetti, Underwood Corporation, and others. The Preface and Part I, "The

Corporate Scene," should be read by anyone undertaking or thinking about undertaking an identity program.

David E. Carter's *Corporate Identity Manuals*[3] is a compilation of thirteen manuals, including those of such firms as Liggett Group, McGraw Edison, Pitney-Bowes, and Sherwin-Williams. While Carter's work is not so analytical as Rosen's, nor so penetrating in the philosophy and objectives of identity programs, it presents a view of corporate identity from the broad perspective of the thirteen reprinted manuals.

Two other references, compilations of trademarks and symbols, illustrate a vast range of design trademarks. These are Barbara Baer Capitman's *American Trademark Designs*[4] and Yasaburo Kuwayama's two-volume work *Trademarks and Symbols*.[5] The first of Kuwayama's volumes treats designs based on letters of the alphabet; the second treats symbolic designs.

Within these four references, one may see examples of identity programs and trademark designs by hundreds of design firms, including the work of outstanding contemporary practitioners such as Saul Bass/Herb Yager and Associates; Walter Landor Associates; Anspach, Grossman, Portugal; Gertsman and Meyers; Gregory Fossella Associates; Lippincott and Margulies; Morton Goldsholl Associates; Chermayeff and Geismar; Pentagram Design; Henrion Design Associates; and Schecter and Partners, to name but a few of the largest and best known. The American Institute of Graphic Arts, the Art Directors Club, or the Industrial Designers Society of America can be of help in locating a design firm that suits your needs.

Selecting a Design Firm

Selecting a design firm is quite akin to hiring a new employee for a specialized job. Interview several such firms and see what they offer and how well their offerings meet your needs. You should explore your program with perhaps five or six different design firms initially.

In your initial interviews with prospective firms, almost invariably one of the first questions they will ask is what are your objectives. What do you want to accomplish through a corporate identity program? The answers may not be easy, but a clear-cut statement of your objectives is important and helpful to the prospective designer, and as a guideline to your committee. Do you wish to appear as a modern, youth-oriented clothing company? An international company offering a wide variety of leisure-time products? A solid, community-oriented chain of general merchandise retail outlets? A substantial firm of financial experts offering investment advice and counsel to small and large investors alike? Do you want a subdued appearance or one that stands out from the crowd? Do you want to appear large or small, national, international, local, or none of these? Do you wish to appear reserved or forward looking? The design firm will ask searching questions to find out how you want to appear before the public. What *are* your corporate identity and image objectives?

After your initial interviews with several design firms, you face the job of selecting two, three, or four to make formal proposals for the identity program you wish to undertake. The design firm's proposal is a prospectus of its approach to your problem, usually including an oral presentation to your committee, illustrated with examples of the firm's work for other clients. I am unaware of any design firm that insists on payment for a proposal. But as the design firm's cost of preparing a proposal can be significant, select your firms with care. In fairness to them, choose only likely prospects. As already stated, limit the number to no more than three or four. Beyond that, the proposals all begin to sound and look the same; you only create confusion within your committee by asking a dozen or more firms for proposals.

Usually the proposals offer a program with a minimum of three stages, each of which requires a separate contract: the audit or familiarization stage, concluding with an analysis and broad recommendations; the design concept stage; and the total final program. Additional stages may include full-scale mockups and working models of architectural and mechanical items, and supervision by the designer of program implementation, including preparation of the corporate identity manual.

Depending on company size and geography, an audit or familiarization may require from a week to several months to complete. During this stage, the designer becomes almost an employee of the company, probing its objectives, examining its business attitudes and philosophies, studying existing identification and the company's equity in it, learning the chain of command, studying its methods of marketing and the specialized aspects of its operations, acquiring some knowledge of its history, and looking at its previous efforts in graphics and product design. The designer observes competition and talks to management, sales personnel, and customers. He may collect samples of company business papers, catalogs, packages, and promotional items and ask for samples of current and past advertising and photographs of company facilities. If the facilities are widely dispersed, he may visit several, observing, photographing, and discussing almost every aspect of the visual identity. This is the period during which the designer acquires company orientation and a feeling for what is good about the existing visual identity and what might well be improved or replaced. His audit report to the client company's identification committee summarizes his findings and suggests what might be done to refurbish or replace the visual identity.

In the second stage—the development of design concepts— the designer applies to the problem his skills and experience, his knowledge of the client and the client's objectives, and his imagination and relentless effort as well as the imagination and effort of his staff. He and the highly trained and skilled artists, designers, and marketing specialists that comprise his staff may prepare hundreds of sketches and draft dozens of concepts. It is a time for burning midnight oil at the design firm's headquarters. Through the processes of review, selection, and rejection, including many tests that sample possible public reaction to various ideas, the designer and his staff arrive at a concept for the client's visual identity. Sometimes one or two alternative and quite different solutions to the problem are prepared. These are presented to the client as text and sketches drawn in dozens of ways and in a variety of applications to meet the identity objectives.

The last stage of the three-part program is the design firm's refinement and detailed preparation of the concept selected as the result of the second stage. It is impractical to list here the myriad details to which the designer must attend and that must be coordinated as integral parts of the visual identity. No point or element of the identity can be left to chance if the designer is to fulfill his obligations and commitment to the client.

The program staging will be outlined by the design firm in its initial proposal. Each stage of the design firm's work may be a separate contract for which you are entitled to know the charges, the time required, and what you are receiving. You should agree, too, on confidentiality, exclusivity, and ownership of materials. All these conditions should be clearly stated in the contract. Confidentiality is ingrained in reputable design firms. Even so, put it in writing. Exclusivity simply means the designer agrees not to undertake an identity program for your competitors while working for you and for six months (sometimes longer) after completing your assignment; otherwise he would have a conflict of interests. The contract usually also specifies that upon completion of the design firm's work, its report and all materials related to it are to be turned over to the client and become the client's exclusive property. A provision may be included that the designer may keep copies for his files and use portions of it to illustrate the quality of the firm's services. Some clients prefer to store the design work with the designer for safekeeping and call for items as needed. This helps prevent loss of and damage to fragile work.

Your reasons for selecting one firm from three or four candidates will be both objective and subjective. You may find one firm's previous work quite impressive and just the sort of thing you are looking for. Its reputation may be outstanding and may appeal to your appreciation for a high degree of professionalism. Or that firm's charge and time schedule may appear more attractive than another's, and better suited to your budget. It is a good idea to ask for references of satisfied clients and the names of individuals within the client firm with whom the designer has worked closely, and to check with them. Does the design firm perform as promised? Does it meet the schedules it outlines? Are cost estimates fairly accurate or will you be confronted with unexpected charges for unexpected services? Does the design firm appear to limit its work load to the capacity of its staff, or does it seem to take on so much at any one time that its work appears to be rushed and its staff overworked?

Do you feel you can work comfortably, confidently, and confidentially with members of the design firm for a year or two? Is the firm well established and relatively steady and complete, or will it have to hire temporary help to do your job? Is the firm in a state of reorganization, which may possibly dilute the attention given to your project? Some design firms are one-, two-, or three-person operations that either fill out the staff on a temporary basis for a particular job, or subcontract portions of it. Other firms are complete with marketing analysts, expert designers, artists, draftsmen, and photographers, and they have all the other skills and disciplines for any type of assignment. Both types of firms are capable of excellent work. However, you should be aware of and take into account the inside structure of the firm you engage as a possible factor in your working relationships.

Costs

A new visual identity program can be as elaborate and costly as you wish to make it, although the success of the program is not necessarily related to either. Some costly and elaborate programs have fizzled, while inexpensive and simple programs have been highly successful. It works both ways.

Contracts usually call for a fixed fee plus expenses. If your company is international in scope, the largest item of the design firm's expense may be travel and living expenses associated with the audit. Also included as expense items are long-distance telephone charges, messenger services, photography, typography, special art work, and other outside costs incurred for the study. These expenses may be billed to you by the designer either at actual cost or at cost with a 15 percent service charge added—a common practice. To avoid the surcharge, costs may be billed directly to the client. However, for a large program involving many expense items from many sources, handling numerous invoices and obtaining the necessary authorizations and approval signatures for payment might prove more trouble than it is worth. If all expense charges were billed or routed to the client by the designer, with his surcharge added, the client could at least determine readily the costs associated with the identity program and turn to the designer to resolve billing ambiguities or questions of charges.

Be certain you understand just how far the contract you are signing extends. At the outset of the program, the contract usually covers only the first or audit stage, with no further commitment on your part. The expense of the audit is only a part of the total cost of a total program. Depending on how elaborate the program is to be, additional stages can be as costly as or more costly than the audit stage. Usually, the design firm is reluctant at the outset to estimate or even guess the total cost—so much depends on the outcome of the first-stage audit. However, after the designer's total fees and costs are in place, there is one thing to remember. A good design firm will recommend things you should continue to do based on sound marketing practice. If you are not doing these things, there may be hidden losses far in excess of the one-time costs of a new identity program. The costs of the program can be amortized over ten to twenty years.

Working with the Design Firm

After selecting a firm and signing a contract, provide full cooperation without interfering or meddling. There are two facets of the program that a committee should recognize in particular as vulnerable to its hasty reactions.

On completion of the second stage of the program, the designer presents his concepts to the committee as sketches. Because of the technical expertise of the design firm, the sketched art may appear complete and finished to the committee. Committee members fail to appreciate the additional effort needed to refine and coordinate a host of artistic and mechanical details necessary for bringing the program to fruition. Any committee that believes the stage-two sketches are adequate for its purposes almost certainly dooms the program to failure.

The second point of particular vulnerability occurs when the company with a new design program in progress becomes impatient to apply its new mark or other parts of the program before the study is completed. This is self-defeating, because it tends to freeze design thinking. Moreover, fragmenting the program greatly reduces the impact of introducing it as a unit in an orderly fashion. For greatest benefit, public introduction of the *total* program should be carefully planned and timed.

As program development progresses, avoid at all costs bringing in friends or relatives to help with decisions or to interject their ideas. You may want their opinions as outsiders, which is fine, but interference with the program or work of the design firm—never.

One professional designer was the victim of such interference. He had spent months working on the design concepts and preparing the visuals for an identification study, at no small expense to the client. Included were working drawings and art for the layout and furnishings of the plant reception area, the executive offices, and the company cafeteria—the colors, furnishings, the lighting, and the wall decorations. All were part of an integrated, total corporate design program. At this stage, the designer was told that the company president's wife was adding her own touches to the designs! She had bought landscaped wallpaper, selected paint and carpeting, and was busy buying furniture, relying on the expertise gained at an evening course in decoration at the local adult education school.

Friends, relatives, and self-styled experts fail almost totally to grasp the depth and significance of a corporate identity program. If you engage a professional designer, let him or her be a professional designer all the way. Your enthusiastic support will be the most rewarding gesture you can make.

You should have within your company one person to act as liaison with the design firm. Questions invariably arise, as do needs for specific reference materials. It is unfair to the design firm, and wastes a lot of its valuable time at your expense, to expect it to rummage through your company either in person or by telephone seeking what it needs. Give the designer one name and phone number, preferably the name of an employee of several years' service and broad company experience, who knows where to obtain the requested materials or where to find answers to the designer's questions.

Once at work, a design firm usually wishes to be left alone to attack the problem without client interference. Cooperate with the firm, supply what it needs, and answer its questions, but don't needle it for status reports or interrupt it for "just a peek at what you've done so far." All will come in due course, and in an orderly fashion.

Special Considerations at the Outset

An important aspect of a corporate identity program concerns those corporations having diverse operations and several scattered plants and offices, each carrying its own identification and using its own trademarks. One objective of an identity program might be to provide one unified corporate "look" to all these units, either subverting or removing the unit individuality in favor of a family identity.

However, before such a change is undertaken, the consequences must be weighed carefully. Company brand identity and loyalty in certain cases may be much more important than parent firm identification or a unified corporate appearance. The situation calls for expert consideration and a careful probe of the equities in the existing identifications and trademarks of the separate units making up the corporation. It is a policy decision for top management.

One solution to this type of problem is to retain the existing identities of the various units and add a corporate signature or trademark to the individual identities. A familiar example is the appearance of the Borden emblem on packages of a wide variety of products made by separately identified and disparate Borden units.

A further aspect of this type of problem is that of a company undertaking an identity change involving various offices and plants in foreign countries. National pride may rebel against overt association with a firm based in another country. It may be quite damaging to change a company name long associated with origins or roots in France or Sweden or Brazil, for example, to identification with The Jones Group, headquartered in New York or Chicago. Investigate not only the possible unfavorable reactions to a name change, but also possible legal and tax problems. As a firm based in the United States operating in a foreign country and identified as such under your new identity program, you may find you have a different tax structure from before, when the foreign company was recognized as a local operation with some owners outside the country.

The problems discussed here boil down to a single consideration: where does the greatest advantage lie? Will a monolithic identification system bring greater overall advantages in the long term, or will it be more advantageous to provide regional or unit individuality? This is a high-management policy decision that should be resolved at the outset of the program. The services and advice of a marketing consultant should be considered.

Factors for a Successful Program

The success of a new corporate identity program depends on many important factors. Perhaps foremost is the complete commitment and backing of the highest management levels within your company. This does not mean total agreement with everything the design firm proposes. It means dedication to the goal of a new identity. The chief executive officers of the company must support the undertaking 100 percent. They must be kept informed of progress and their votes or opinions invited at crucial decision stages. If planning one or more extra initial presentations by the design firm will help build the rationale and gain top-level support, by all means do so. A program without that support is doomed. Moreover, perhaps nothing is so defeating or so demoralizing to a design firm as to learn after months of hard work that the client's top management either is only vaguely aware of the program or is highly skeptical of its possible outcome or benefits.

The design firm's solution to your problem is, of course, a key element of success. If you have selected the firm carefully, its offerings should fulfill the identity program objectives established at the outset, or should provide solutions to the problem. The design firm's recommendations must be reviewed in a highly objective manner. It is not so important to *like* the recommendations as it is to agree that they are right in relation to the problems to be solved or the objectives to be met. Aesthetics need not be abandoned, but the problem is fundamentally a marketing one rather than one of pure artistry. Members of the company identity committee who consider themselves something of an artist must subordinate their artistic opinions to the realities of the marketplace and the expertise of the design firm.

The working relationship between the design firm and the client may not always run smoothly. It may become apparent after one or two presentations that the designer's ideas or working methods are unsuitable or not at all what was expected. One recourse is to terminate your relationship with the firm at the end of stage one or stage two and start over. You won't have lost everything, because you have the audit report and at least some idea of what you don't like—which should make it easier to zero in on your preferences in a much shorter time. If you decide to retain the design firm, don't hesitate to send it back to the drawing boards.

A new or modernized trademark may very likely be the heart of your new identity program and could well prove to be the most difficult point for agreement between you and the designer. Disagreement probably would stem not from incompetence on the part of the designer, but rather from reluctance on the part of your management to give up that fine old trademark that has served so well for fifty years. A sensitive design firm will try hard to keep your existing mark or a recognizable modification of it if there is indeed great equity in it. A design firm that favors change for the sake of change may not be focused on the goal. Changing your corporate signature so that people in your universe no longer recognize it is a serious matter, which is made no easier to accept because your design firm has numerous graphic awards to its credit. Your interests must be served first.

Design firms take pride in their work and have a reputation to maintain. They are not interested in lowering their professional standards just to satisfy a client. It accrues to their benefit, as well as to the benefit of their clients, to produce superior work. Therefore don't burden the designer with sacred cows. If an old symbol must remain within your identity program, let all potential design firms—those you interview—know this at the outset. They may then decide either to withdraw from consideration or to work around your requirements. You will be far better off in the long run to retire all sacred cows to the company museum. Otherwise, you may be disappointed in the overall results, reflecting fresh paint on a tired façade.

Do not, under any circumstances, permit in-house tampering with the design firm's work or recommendations. For example, the designer will probably come up with a new set of uniform letterheads and business cards as a part of the new identity. You may expect at least one staff member or official of your company to be affronted that his or her letterhead and business card will now look the same as all others. That official once had a unique set that in his or her opinion reflected a higher staff position. But so did every other officer, and this variety of designs eroded the appearance that they all served the same company. Our friend again seeks "status" stationery with designs remote from the new specifications. Don't give in. Convince that official or staff member to use what you have paid for—a corporate identity, not a conglomerate of individual identities.

Be candid with the design firm. Give it all the material and information to work with that you can. Let the designers decide what is important and what is trivial. As one design firm owner stated, "We would rather have too much to work with than too little. We can sort it out."

Finally, the end of the designer's work—the complete program—is just the beginning of yours. Even if you retain the firm to supervise the implementation, the onus of making the program work is still on your company.

Launching the Program

Launching an identity program is a matter of carefully planning, prescribing, and scheduling every detail to be changed and every new item to be introduced. The plans and schedules should be developed with the design firm so that the new identity will unfold to the public as a logical entity rather than as a spasmodic or haphazard change.

It is important to advise employees and stockholders of impending changes before public announcement. If during the development stages secrecy has been maintained, as it should be, most employees and certainly all nonemployee stockholders will be unaware of the new program. It is advisable to hold one or more employee meetings to explain the reasons for the change and the extent of it. At the least, a general memo from the company president or board chairman to all employees briefly describing the new program and its importance is of great help and value in obtaining cooperation and maintaining high morale. Similarly, a special early report to stockholders and possibly to company annuitants should be considered.

Large companies with literally thousands of identity points to be changed should start planning and scheduling months in advance of the date for public introduction of the new identity. Even though details and specifications for the new identity may not be available, the items to be changed, their locations, and the quantity involved should be listed and priorities assigned. Instruction sheets must be prepared for field use. It may be necessary to prepare manuals detailing engineering changes needed to accommodate new signs. News releases and announcements through advertising in printed media, radio, and television must be prepared.

If the designer is retained to implement the program, his or her firm will prepare most of the specification and instruction sheets or manuals. Nevertheless, there inevitably will be items requiring changes that your company must resolve and handle. Nothing should be left to chance or to instructions to the field to "do the best you can with it."

Once the design work is finished and your program is launched, stick to it until it is in place. Give one person or office in your company the authority to say yes or no to the inevitable requests for variations or exceptions and to make the decision stick.

Keep at the implementation until your new identity is in place. Stay on schedule. Don't dawdle or be indecisive. If your company is small, you may be able to accomplish wonders quickly. One company consisting of a small and relatively local chain of gasoline service stations delivered to each of its outlets all the materials and equipment for a well-planned identification change. Each station received new signs, new gasoline pumps and paint, plus instructions and a time schedule. Beginning on a Friday and working almost around the clock, a completely new identity was presented to customers throughout the network on Monday morning. At the other end of the scale, a large national oil company required nearly a year of closely coordinated work before all its various units, outlets, and operations were reidentified under a new program.

Schedule your changes for maximum effect and keep at it until complete. If you procrastinate, the incentives and momentum are lost and interest dies. Budgets may become snarled. Five years after starting your program, you may find your identity in worse shape than before.

If your company is dispersed geographically, even within a relatively small area, do not take for granted the proper implementation of your new identity by means of directives from the head office. Manuals, instruction sheets, and specifications are not enough. A visit to each location is essential not only to inspect progress and results, but also to impress on the various units the importance of rigorous adherence to exact specifications. If the various units need a local identity, the design firm should include plans for it in the overall program. Without specified local identifiers, if needed, the *corporate* identity may become fractured through local designs locally conceived. Visits to each location will uncover such needs or presumed needs (if undiscovered by the audit), or will forestall indiscriminate tampering with the system. Firmness may be needed to bring about removal of newly applied local "art" that is at odds with the overall identity program.

The Corporate Visual Identity Manual

A well-constructed corporate visual identity manual is a must. It is the central reference, the authority, and the guide for all applications of your identity program. It is a specifications and standards book for the trademarks, colors, styles of type, and designs and their applications. It may be a four-page leaflet, a forty-page manual, or a 400-page document.

If you have working drawings and specifications from the design firm and use them to put your new identity into place, why then do you need a manual? Primarily, it is for the future, the record of what is done today for use as the company grows. Five years after your program was implemented, it would be virtually impossible without a manual to go back and reconstruct the decisions made at the beginning. A manual not only provides this record, but if properly revised as needs arise, serves as the latest corporate word on identification.

Saul Bass, one of today's leading graphics and industrial designers, believes an identity manual should be more than a set of specifications. It should be a teaching instrument, an exposition of identification purpose and philosphy as applied to the particular program. As a teaching instrument, the manual should convey the sense and feeling of the identity program. It should instill in the employees responsible for it the complete picture of the system as a corporate entity rather than a collection of parts.

With passing time, the responsibility for corporate identification passes to others. It is important that they know the thinking

and philosophy behind the identity program. Otherwise there may
be a tendency to tamper with or to modify the program, to make
"improvements" in it or to extend the system to applications for
which it was never intended or designed. An identification manual
designed as the corporate authority, as a teaching instrument, and
as a set of standards and specifications will be of value to your
program far beyond the cost of its preparation.

At the *user* end of the manual, users have sometimes said,
"All I want is to be told exactly what goes where. I don't care why.
Spare me the sermons. I'm much too busy to have to study ten
pages of a manual to find out whether I put up a red circle or a
blue square, or whether the letterhead is to be printed with green
or black ink." The obvious answer to this attitude is to construct
the corporate identity manual both as a specification book and as
a teaching instrument. The full text is provided to key offices and
staff members responsible for the full program. Separate sheets or
sections can be provided as application instructions to the various
units and people concerned.

A Final Word

A corporate identity program cannot be undertaken lightly. It
cannot be said too often that it is a job for professionals, who must
be supported wholeheartedly by company officials but not inter-
fered with. No facet of identity can be overlooked, from the manner in which your firm's name and trademark is displayed in the
yellow pages of telephone directories to their appearance in the
largest signs. All are pieces making up your corporate visual
identity.

A clean, new identity with a well-conceived and well-executed
new trademark will be a source of corporate pride and a major
contribution to a well-perceived and well-accepted corporate
image.

APPENDICES

Appendix 1

Supreme Court Decision Regarding Trademarks

The following is a statement by Mr. Justice Frankfurter in a decision by the Supreme Court of the United States, No. 649, May 4, 1942. *Mishawaka Rubber and Woolen Manufacturing Company* vs *S. S. Kresge*, 53 USPQ 323.

Part of the quotation appears in the beginning of Chapter 3. Because various parts of this segment of the opinion appear in trademark literature, it is presented here in full.

The protection of trade marks is the law's recognition of the psychological function of symbols. If it is true that we live by symbols, it is no less true that we purchase goods by them. A trade mark is a merchandising short-cut which induces a purchaser to select what he wants, or what he has been led to believe he wants. The owner of a mark exploits this human propensity by making every effort to impregnate the atmosphere of the market with the drawing power of a congenial symbol. Whatever the means employed, the aim is the same—to convey through the mark, in the minds of potential customers, the desirability of the commodity upon which it appears. Once established, the trade mark owner has something of value. If another poaches upon the commercial magnetism of the symbol he has created, the owner can obtain legal redress.

Appendix 2A

ZAM Trademark Search

The following pages reproduce the report from an actual trademark search prepared for the author's imaginary ZAM Industries and its product ZAM car polish.

NAME OF MARK

ZAM

CLASSIFICATION SEARCHED

1-4-6-15-16-19-29-52
All Class Exact

DATE

April 25, 1980

CLIENT

Zam Industries

ANALYST

Kathy Cranisky

TRADEMARK: ZAM

GOODS: CAR POLISH.

CLASSES(U.S.): 1-4-6-15-16-19-29-52
               ALL CLASS EXACT

PATENT OFFICE CITATIONS:

ZAM

          CLASS 6
          INT.CL. 5
          FOR ROOM DEODORANT
          OWNER: TABTROL COMPANY, INC., BALTIMORE, MD.
          SN: 236,669   FILED OCTOBER 25, 1979   USE: JULY 3, 1973

RN 431,582. Tabtrol Company, Inc., Baltimore, Md. Filed
Aug. 3, 1972.   CLASS 6
                                           SN: 431,582
          ZAM   PUB FOR OPP APRIL 17, 1973
                                           RN: 962,394   REG JULY 3, 1973
For Diffusion Type Chemical Liquid Preparation for Con-   CANCELLED: JANUARY 8, 1980 SECTION 8
troling Odors (Int. Cl. 5).
First use Mar. 2, 1959.

Ser. No. 592,251. Chemical Service of Baltimore, Balti-   CLASS 52
more, Md. Filed Feb. 10, 1950.   SN: 592,251
          ZAM   PUB FOR OPP JUNE 3, 1952
                                           RN: 563,280   REG AUGUST 26, 1952
For Liquid Chemical Concentrate for Washing Glass-   NOT RENEWED
ware and Dishes.
Claims use since Jan. 24, 1950.

ZAMBRA
          CLASS 52
          INT.CL. 3
          FOR TOILET SOAP
          OWNER: ANTONIO PUIG S.A., BARCELONA, SPAIN
          SN: 67,259   FILED OCTOBER 29, 1975   USE: APRIL 12, 1946
          PUBLISHED FOR OPPOSITION APRIL 27, 1976
          RN: 1,043,914   REGISTERED JULY 20, 1976
          OTHER REG: 861,477
          OTHER REG: SPANISH 153648

                              THIS REPORT INCLUDES THOSE
                              APPLICATIONS, NOT REQUIRING
                              FURTHER PROCESSING, FILED
                              THROUGH DECEMBER 26, 1979

ZOOM WITH DESIGN
        CLASS 52
        INT.CL. 3
        FOR CLEANING PREPARATION IN CRYSTAL FORM TO BE USED FOR RUGS,
            UPHOLSTERY, CLOTHING, AND FOR SURFACES OF FURNITURE, WOODWORK
            AND WALLS
        OWNER: BETTY W. HIRTZIG, D/B/A BANBETT PRODUCTS CO., INGLEWOOD,
            CALIF.
        SN: 316,625   FILED JANUARY 15, 1969   USE: FEBRUARY 20, 1945
        PUBLISHED FOR OPPOSITION OCTOBER 28, 1969
        RN: 884,310 REGISTERED JANUARY 13, 1970
        OTHER REG: 420585

ZEAM
        CLASS 52
        INT.CL. 3
        FOR CHEMICAL CLEANING PREPARATION USED IN STEAM CLEANING PROCESSES
        OWNER: MALTER INTERNATIONAL CORPORATION, D/B/A MALTER INTERNATIONAL,
            NEW ORLEANS, LA.
        SN: 56,123   FILED JUNE 25, 1975   USE: FEBRUARY, 1975
        PUBLISHED FOR OPPOSITION MAY 11, 1976
        RN: 1,045,200 REGISTERED AUGUST 3, 1976

ZAMBUJAL
        CLASS 51-52
        INT.CL. 3
        FOR COLOGNE AND DUSTING POWDER ; TOILET SOAP
        OWNER: AVON PRODUCTS, INC., NEW YORK, NEW YORK
        SN: 333,038   FILED JULY 22, 1969   USE: APRIL 30, 1969
        PUBLISHED FOR OPPOSITION JULY 14, 1970
        RN: 899,837 REGISTERED SEPTEMBER 29, 1970
        CANCELLED: NOVEMBER 30, 1976 SECTION 8

ZAMBRA
        CLASS 52
        INT.CL. 3
        FOR TOILET SOAP
        OWNER: ANTONIO PUIG S.A., BARCELONA, SPAIN.
        SN: 269,450   FILED APRIL 18, 1967
        PUBLISHED FOR OPPOSITION JULY 16, 1968
        RN: 858,072 REGISTERED OCTOBER 1, 1968
        OTHER REG: SPANISH 153648
        CANCELLED: DECEMBER 3, 1974 SECTION 8

ALA KAZAM

        CLASS 52
        INT.CL. 3
        FOR BATH SOAP
        OWNER: SHULTON, INC., CLIFTON, N.J.
        SN: 332,424   FILED JULY 14, 1969   USE: JUNE 25, 1969
        PUBLISHED FOR OPPOSITION FEBRUARY 17, 1970
        RN: 890,629 REGISTERED MAY 5, 1970
        CANCELLED: JULY 6, 1976 SECTION 8

ZOOM

        CLASS 16
        FOR PAINTS
        OWNER: NORRIS PAINT AND VARNISH CO., INC., SALEM, OREG.
        SN: 212,567   FILED FEBRUARY 23, 1965   USE: JULY 3, 1962
        PUBLISHED FOR OPPOSITION MAY 3, 1966
        RN: 811,245 REGISTERED JULY 19, 1966

ZAR

        CLASS 16
        FOR FILM-FORMING COATING MATERIAL TO BE USED FOR THE SAME PURPOSES
           AS VARNISH
        OWNER: UNITED GILSONITE LABORATORIES, SCRANTON, PA
        SN: 83,018   FILED OCTOBER 9, 1959   USE: SEPTEMBER 25, 1959
        PUBLISHED FOR OPPOSITION FEBRUARY 16, 1960
        RN: 696,989 REGISTERED MAY 3, 1960

Z A P

        CLASS 52
        INT.CL. 3
        FOR CARPET CLEANING CHEMICAL
        OWNER: ASSOCIATED LABORATORIES, INC., RALEIGH, N.C.
        SN: 161,780   FILED MARCH 13, 1978   USE: FEBRUARY 7, 1978
        PUBLISHED FOR OPPOSITION JANUARY 8, 1980

Z A R

        CLASS 52
        INT.CL. 3
        FOR PAINT AND VARNISH REMOVERS
        OWNER: UNITED GILSONITE LABORATORIES, SCRANTON, PA.
        SN: 194,933   FILED JUNE 4, 1964   USE: MARCH 3, 1964
        PUBLISHED FOR OPPOSITION JANUARY 5, 1965
        RN: 787,294 REGISTERED MARCH 23, 1965
        OTHER REG: 696,989, 717,097, AND 717,098
        AFFADAVIT SECTION 8-15 APRIL 27, 1970

ZOOM
CLASS 6-52
FOR A HEAVY DUTY STEAM CLEANER, SAFE ON ALL STEEL AND ALUMINUM
SURFACES, WILL NOT DAMAGE PAINTED SURFACES
OWNER: MALTER INTERNATIONAL CORPORATION, NEW ORLEANS, LA.
SN: 434,129   FILED AUGUST 30, 1972   USE: NOVEMBER 4, 1965
ABANDONED: OCTOBER 1974

ZOOM
CLASS 52
INT.CL. 3
FOR ALKALINE BLEND CONCRETE CLEANER
OWNER: NATIONAL CHEMSEARCH CORPORATION, IRVING, TEX.
SN: 33,266   FILED SEPTEMBER 30, 1974   USE: JANUARY 25, 1963
ABANDONED: MAY 1976

Z A S
CLASS 52
INT.CL. 3
FOR LIQUID CLEANER FOR GENERAL HOUSEHOLD USAGE
OWNER: VILLA CHEMICAL INTERNATIONAL, INC., CORPUS CHRISTI, TEX.
SN: 321,421   FILED MARCH 11, 1969   USE: DECEMBER 4, 1968
PUBLISHED FOR OPPOSITION DECEMBER 9, 1969
RN: 886,865   REGISTERED FEBRUARY 24, 1970
CANCELLED: APRIL 27, 1976 SECTION 8

ZAT WITH DESIGN
CLASS 4
FOR AUTOMOBILE, TRUCK, BUS AND MOTORCYCLE POLISH AND GLAZE
OWNER: JOSEPH A. HALLIHAN, D/B/A ZAT PRODUCTS CO., CHERRY VALLEY,
MASS.
SN: 355,647   FILED APRIL 1, 1970   USE: AUGUST 29, 1969
PUBLISHED FOR OPPOSITION NOVEMBER 3, 1970
RN: 906,071   REGISTERED JANUARY 19, 1971
CANCELLED: MARCH 15, 1977 SECTION 8

ZIM
CLASS 52
FOR ORGANIC SOLVENT CLEANER-NAMELY, PINE OIL CONTAINING CASTOR OIL
DERIVED FROM STEAM DISTILLATION OF PINE TREE RESIDUES AND
USED AS A CLEANING SOLVENT.
OWNER: CASTOLEUM CORPORATION, C.B.A. THE CASTOLEUM CORPORATION,
YONKERS, N.Y.
SN: 247,006   FILED JUNE 1, 1966   USE: MARCH, 1941
PUBLISHED FOR OPPOSITION JANUARY 24, 1967
RN: 827,314   REGISTERED APRIL 11, 1967
CANCELLED: JUNE 5, 1973 SECTION 8

ZIP WITH DESIGN
        CLASS 52
        FOR CLEANER
        OWNER: CASTOLEUM CORPORATION, YONKERS, N.Y.
        SN: 127,091   FILED SEPTEMBER 1, 1961   USE: DECEMBER 15, 1958
        ABANDONED: FEBRUARY 1966

A M WITH DESIGN
        CLASS 4
        FOR RUBBING, BUFFING AND POLISHING COMPOUNDS; LIQUID AND PASTE
            WAXES
        OWNER: AUTO WAX COMPANY, INC., DALLAS, TEXAS
        SN: 335,184   FILED AUGUST 13, 1969   USE: MARCH 25, 1964
        PUBLISHED FOR OPPOSITION JUNE 8, 1971
        RN: 918,735   REGISTERED AUGUST 24, 1971

A M
        CLASS 6-15-52
        FOR BOILER COMPOUNDS, RUST AND CORROSION INHIBITORS ; FUEL OIL
            ADDITIVES ; SLUDGE, RUST, SCALE AND CORROSION CLEANING AND
            REMOVING PREPARATIONS
        OWNER: ALKEN-MURRAY CORPORATION, NEW YORK, N.Y.
        SN: 213,510   FILED MARCH 8, 1965   USE: JUNE 15, 1964
        PUBLISHED FOR OPPOSITION SEPTEMBER 13, 1966
        RN: 819,335   REGISTERED NOVEMBER 29, 1966

A M WITH DESIGN
        CLASS 52
        INT.CL. 3
        FOR SOLVENTS FOR REMOVING WAX, TAR, AND ADHESIVES; AUTOMOBILE
            BUMPER CLEANER; SOAP TO REMOVE BUGS FROM AUTOMOBILE HOODS AND
            GRILLS; GLASS CLEANER, WHITE SIDEWALL TIRE CLEANER AND MOTOR
            CLEANER; SOAP TO DISSOLVE GREASE AND DIRT IN CHAMOIS SKINS;
            CAR WASH IN POWDERED AND LIQUID FORM; CLEANING COMPOUND FOR
            USE IN PRESSURE STEAM MACHINES; UPHOLSTERY SHAMPOO,
            COMBINATION FABRIC DYE AND SHAMPOO; AND SPOT REMOVER
        OWNER: AUTO WAX COMPANY, INC., DALLAS, TEXAS
        SN: 335,187   FILED AUGUST 13, 1969   USE: FEBRUARY 25, 1964
        PUBLISHED FOR OPPOSITION JUNE 1, 1971
        RN: 918,689   REGISTERED AUGUST 17, 1971

ALIKA ZAM
    CLASS 52   FOR GENERAL ALL PURPOSE CLEANER
    OWNER: PROFESSIONAL FUND RAISERS, INC., KNOXVILLE, TN.
    STATE: TENNESSEE
    REG DATE: FEBRUARY 14, 1972

ZAMS FAMOUS FOR NOTHING
    CLASS 100   FOR MISCELLANEOUS
    OWNER: FLOYD SAMUEL HAGANS,PO.BOX 106 PORT BOLIVAR, TEXAS
    STATE: TEXAS
    REG DATE: JANUARY 18, 1973

WE HAVE CAREFULLY ATTEMPTED TO ACQUIRE ALL STATE TRADEMARKS AND HAVE, TO THE
BEST OF OUR ABILITY, DONE SO. HOWEVER, BECAUSE OF THE CONDITION OF MANY OF THESE
FILES AND THE DIFFICULTIES INHERENT IN DEALING REMOTELY WITH ALL 50 STATES,
THERE MAY BE ERRORS. WE THEREFORE SUGGEST YOU CHECK WITH THE APPROPRIATE
SECRETARY OF STATE'S OFFICE WHEN THE STATUS OF A MARK OF INTEREST IS IN DOUBT.

am/wm

INVOICE #   49,888

SEARCH: ZAM

Common Law

ZAN KLEEN   Zanin & Son, Inc., Weehawken, NJ
Thomas Register Of American Manufacturers - 1980

ZAR (paint & varnish remover) United Gilsonite Labs., Scranton, PA
National Paint, Varnish and Lacquer Association - 1976 & 1978 Supplement

ZAP (all purpose cleaners) American Manufacturing Co., Atlanta, GA
National Paint, Varnish and Lacquer Association - 1976 & 1978 Supplement

Trade Names

ZAM CHEMICAL CORPORATION, 1000 Harbor Street, Pittsburg, CA

ZAM ENTERPRISES, 448 Harvard, Houston, TX

ZAM MANUFACTURING INC., 6061 Telegraph Road, Toledo, OH

Z A M ENTERPRISES INC., 1620 Emerson, Evanston, IL

184

Appendix 2B

Analysis of the ZAM Search Report*

The preceding is a copy of the ZAM Search Report prepared by TCR Service, Inc. As mentioned in Chapter 5, ZAM car polish and ZAM Industries are fictions created for illustrative purposes. The search report and the marks and companies listed are genuine.

In considering the report, keep in mind that the fictional ZAM car polish would be sold in service stations, supermarkets, variety and hardware stores, and automotive supply stores. Consequently, it is necessary to search for any identical existing mark or one similar to it or suggestive of ZAM likely to appear on car polish, on other types of polish or cleaners such as for furniture, on any types of products for automotive maintenance sold in retail outlets, or on products that would appear in the same types of outlets, especially in outlet sections displaying the same and related goods. Under such situations, customers would be likely to assume that the products were all from the same source because of the same or similar trademarks, and the use of ZAM on car polish would very probably be eliminated.

The classes of goods searched (report title page) for any mark identical to or suggestive of ZAM are the prior U.S. classification numbers given in the table on the next page.

*The ZAM Search Report was reviewed by a trademark attorney, who provided these analytical comments.

Class	Type of Goods	Class	Type of Goods
1	raw or partly prepared materials	6	chemicals and chemical compositions
4	abrasives and polishing materials (This is the U.S. class of major concern for car polish. Such materials are included in international class 3.)	15	oils and greases
		16	protective and decorative coatings
		19	vehicles
		29	brooms, brushes, and dusters
		52	detergents and soaps

Missing from the list is class 21, "electrical apparatus, machines, and supplies," which includes many of the automotive accessory items sold in the same outlets as car polish. A class 21 search should be ordered.

All remaining classes were searched for ZAM alone ("All Class Exact"); that is, words not identical to but similar to or suggestive of ZAM were not searched in the other classes.

Examination of the search shows no reported existing use of ZAM on car polish. A number of ZAM or similar marks are reported as "canceled," "not renewed," or "abandoned" and need not be considered further unless they are listed in the Common Law search (penultimate page of the report), which they are not. (The fact that a *registration* has been canceled, abandoned, or not renewed is not conclusive evidence that the mark is not in use and therefore available. The owner of the mark might still be using it without registration, and the mark would be protected under common law. If so, the mark should show up in the Common Law section of the report.)

ZAP, page 3, for carpet cleaning chemical, if it is packaged and sold for cleaning carpets or upholstery in automobiles, might deter use of ZAM. Specific trademark uses of ZAP should be checked further.

Three A M trademarks, page 5 of the report, and especially the first and the third, may present problems for ZAM. It will be necessary to examine packages and advertising for A M products to determine whether confusion with ZAM would be likely. For example, it is possible through pure chance that the ZAM packages and the A M packages are confusingly similar in appearance, suggesting that ZAM Industries simply modified the A M packages by adding the letter Z. While this might not eliminate the use of ZAM as a trademark, it would at least require a redesign of ZAM car polish packages and the manner in which the mark is displayed.

Under the Common Law report, the full nature of ZAN KLEEN and of ZAP products is not indicated. These products might be automotive, and should be checked as possible ZAM conflicts.

Under Trade Names, four ZAM companies are listed. The products of any one or of all might include a car polish or related automotive supplies. Hence a check should be made to determine the nature of the companies and their products. Reports such as those available from Dun and Bradstreet usually provide the necessary information.

In summary, while the use of ZAM on car polish appears to be without conflict, it is not certain. Additional checking into existing marks and trade names is necessary.

When the possibility of trademark conflict exists, no matter how remote it may appear to be, always consider how your proposed mark might be received by other companies or by competition. ZAM Industries should consider: "If we were any other company and were owners of any of the trademarks shown in the search report, would we object or have good reason to object if ZAM car polish were to appear on the market?" The answer could be a major factor in deciding whether to adopt ZAM as a trademark.

Appendix 3

Sources for Lists
of Trademarks and Trade Names

The following is but a partial list of the many references listing trademarks, "brands" or "brand names," and trade names. Many trade associations or professional organizations, in their periodicals or journals, annually publish lists of trademarks and trade names related to the products or services of interest to their members. Some of these are indicated here.

Titles of the numerous lists vary—"Trademark Index," "Brand Name Index," "Index of Trade Names," and so on. Essentially all are lists of "trademarks" as defined in the text. Most do not illustrate graphic trademarks. The specialized nature of many of the lists is indicated by the title or by the source.

The Trademark Register of the United States

Published annually. Limited to registered trademarks, listed by registration classes. Shows with each the date of registration and the registration number, but not the specific goods or the owner.

The Trademark Register, 422 Washington Building, Washington, D.C. 20005.

Trademark Stylesheet

The United States Trademark Association publishes "Trademark Stylesheet," each edition of which lists trademarks applicable

to a specific type of goods: Grocery, Textiles, Food Preparation
Appliances and Utensils, etc. Trademarks are listed and the product on which they are applied is indicated. Does not show the
owner of the mark or registration status.

The USTA, 6 East 45th Street, New York, N.Y. 10017.

Thomas Register of American Manufacturers

Published annually. One of the several volumes contains a
Trademark Index to several thousand trademarks, largely for in-
dustrially related products, indicating the nature of the product or
service and the company. Registration status not indicated. See
also "Brand Name" section of *Thomas Grocery Register*.

Thomas Publishing Company, One Penn Plaza, New York,
N.Y. 10001.

Trade Names Dictionary

Second edition, 1979. Over 130,000 entries of trademarks and
trade names for consumer-oriented products, with product description, name of manufacturer or distributor, and other information. Includes an extensive list of source references to trademark
lists. In two volumes.

Gale Research Company, Book Tower, Detroit, Mich. 48226.

New Trade Names

1980 and 1981 Supplements to *Trade Name Dictionary*.
Gale Research Co., as above.

Consumer Sourcebook

Second edition, 1978. Six major sections in two volumes. The
fourth section is a directory of over 17,000 companies providing
consumer goods and services with their brand names.

Gale Research Co., as above.

MacRae's Blue Book

Published annually. Similar to *Thomas Register*. One of several volumes includes a "Trade Name" section—"A ready refer-

ence listing of leading trade names, trade marks and special brand names used by American industry."
MacRae's Blue Book, Hinsdale, Ill. 60521.

Trademark Directory

Issued by the Trademark Bureau, National Paint and Coatings Association, Inc., 1500 Rhode Island Avenue, N.W., Washington, D.C. 20005.

Trade Names of Man-Made Fibers

Appendix 3 in *Introduction to Fibers and Fabrics*, by E. Kornreich. Second edition, 1966, published by American Elsevier Publishing Company.

Drug Topics Red Book—
The Pharmacist's Guide to Products and Prices

Published annually.
Medical Economics Co., Oradell, N.J. 07649.

American Druggist Blue Book

Published annually.
The Hearst Corporation, 224 W. 57th Street, New York, N.Y. 10019.

Commercial Names and Sources

Lists over 14,500 materials by "commercial name, generic type, and manufacturer."
The International Plastics Selector, Inc., San Diego, Calif. 92110.

NPN Factbook

Published annually by National Petroleum News. Includes list of brand names applied to automotive fuels and crankcase oils.

McGraw-Hill, 1221 Avenue of the Americas, New York, N.Y. 10020.

Chemical Week Buyer's Guide Issue

Published annually. Includes lists of "Chemical Tradenames" and "Packaging Tradenames," showing the trademark, the material to which it is applied, and the owner.

McGraw-Hill, 1221 Avenue of the Americas, New York, N.Y. 10020.

U.K. Trade Names

Fourth edition, 1972. Over 70,000 trademarks and trade names in use in the United Kingdom. Shows trademark, product type, and name and address of manufacturer. Some illustrations.

Kompass Publishers Limited, Croydon, England.

Annual Buyers Guide

Package Engineering.
Cahners Publishing Company, Chicago, Ill.

Handbook of Material Trade Names

By O. T. Zimmerman and Irvin Levine. Published 1960 by Industrial Research Services, Dover, New Hampshire.

Jewelers Brand Name and Trademark Guide

600 Third Avenue, New York, N.Y. 10016.

1979 Trademark Design Register

About 13,500 designs, logos, and symbols reproduced in black and white, arranged alphabetically by included letters of words, or, if without letters or words, then within the overall order by name of the company or individual owning the mark. Indexed both by name of manufacturer or owner and by key words and design descriptions. Ninety-nine percent of the marks are registered in the U.S. Patent and Trademark Office. This book does not show the class or classes of goods for which the marks are registered. Published by The Trademark Register, 454 Washington Building, Washington, D.C. 20005.

American Trademark Designs

By Barbara Baer Capitman. "A survey with 732 marks, logos and corporate identity symbols." Trademarks illustrated, owner indicated, and the designer. By categories of goods or services. Published 1976 by Dover Publications, Inc., New York.

Trademarks and Symbols of the World

By Yusaku Kamekura. Illustrates 763 trademarks and trademark designs. Published 1965 by Van Nostrand Reinhold Publishing Company, New York.

Trademarks and Symbols

By Yasaburo Kuwayama. In two volumes, illustrating 1,500 trademarks and symbols. Volume 1—alphabetical designs; Volume 2—symbolic designs. Published 1973 by Van Nostrand Reinhold, New York.

Appendix 4

Prior U.S. Schedule of Classes of Goods and Services   (Titles Only)

Class Title

Goods

1   Raw or partly prepared materials
2   Receptacles
3   Baggage, animal equipments, portfolios, and pocket books
4   Abrasives and polishing materials
5   Adhesives
6   Chemicals and chemical compositions
7   Cordage
8   Smokers' articles, not including tobacco products
9   Explosives, firearms, equipments, and projectiles
10   Fertilizers
11   Inks and inking materials

Class Title

Goods (*continued*)

12   Construction materials
13   Hardware and plumbing and steamfitting supplies
14   Metals and metal castings and forgings
15   Oils and greases
16   Protective and decorative coatings
17   Tobacco products
18   Medicines and pharmaceutical preparations
19   Vehicles
20   Linoleum and oiled cloth
21   Electrical apparatus, machines, and supplies
22   Games, toys, and sporting goods

Class Title

Goods (*continued*)

23 Cutlery, machinery, and tools, and parts thereof

24 Laundry appliances and machines

25 Locks and safes

26 Measuring and scientific appliances

27 Horological instruments

28 Jewelry and precious-metal ware

29 Brooms, brushes, and dusters

30 Crockery, earthenware, and porcelain

31 Filters and refrigerators

32 Furniture and upholstery

33 Glassware

34 Heating, lighting, and ventilating apparatus

35 Belting, hose, machinery packing, and nonmetallic tires

36 Musical instruments and supplies

Class Title

Goods (*continued*)

37 Paper and stationery

38 Prints and publications

39 Clothing

40 Fancy goods, furnishings, and notions

41 Canes, parasols, and umbrellas

42 Knitted, netted, and textile fabrics, and substitutes therefor

43 Thread and yarn

44 Dental, medical, and surgical appliances

45 Soft drinks and carbonated waters

46 Foods and ingredients of foods

47 Wines

48 Malt beverages and liquors

49 Distilled alcoholic liquors

50 Merchandise not otherwise classified

51 Cosmetics and toilet preparations

52 Detergents and soaps

Class	Title	Class	Title
	Services		**Services** (*continued*)
100	Miscellaneous	104	Communication
101	Advertising and business	105	Transportation and storage
102	Insurance and financial	106	Material treatment
103	Construction and repair	107	Education and entertainment

Schedule for certification marks

A. Goods
B. Services

Class Title

Schedule for collective membership marks

200 Collective membership

Notes

Chapter 1

[1] Schecter, Frank I. "The Rational Basis of Trademark Protection," *Harvard Law Review* XL, No. 6, reprinted in *Trademark Reporter* 60, No. 3, May–June 1970.

[2] Lunsford, Julius R., Jr. "Consumers and Trademarks: The Function of Trademarks in the Market Place," *Trademark Reporter* 64, No. 2, March–April 1974, 75.

Chapter 2

[1] Diamond, Sidney. "Untangling the Confusion in Trademark Terminology," *American Bar Association Journal* 65, October 1979, 1523.

[2] Ladas, Stephen P. "Trademark Law," *Encyclopedia Britannica,* 15th ed., Vol. 18, p. 557.

[3] Diamond, Sidney A. *Trademark Problems and How to Avoid Them* (Chicago: Crain Communications, Inc., 1973), p. 1.

[4] McCarthy, J. Thomas. *Trademarks and Unfair Competition* (Rochester, N.Y.: The Lawyers Co-Operative Publishing Co., 1973), p. 108.

[5] The United States Trademark Association, *Glossary* (New York: 1964).

[6] Zinn, Norman H. "Understanding Generic Words," *Trademark Reporter* 63, No. 3, May–June 1973, 173.

[7] Trademark Act of 1946, As Amended. Public Law 489, 79th Congress, Chapter 540. Approved July 5, 1946; 60 Stat. 427 (included in *Trademark Rules of Practice of the Patent and Trademark Office with Forms and Statutes*. U.S. Department of Commerce Patent and Trademark Office, Ninth ed., December 1976, revised May 1979).

Chapter 3

[1] Frankfurter, Felix. *Mishawaka Rubber and Woolen Manufacturing Company* vs *S.S. Kresge Co.* Supreme Court of the United States, No. 649, May 4, 1942. 53 USPQ 323.

[2] McCarthy, J. Thomas. *Trademarks and Unfair Competition* (Rochester, N.Y.: The Lawyers Co-Operative Publishing Co., 1973), pp. 513–66.

[3] Lippincott and Margulies, Inc. *Designing a Brandmark for Today's Marketing* (New York: 1956).

[4] Lunsford, Julius R., Jr. "Consumers and Trademarks: The Function of Trademarks in the Market Place," *Trademark Reporter* 64, No. 2, March–April 1974, 75.

Chapter 4

[1] Lunsford, Julius R., Jr. "The Mechanics and Proof of Secondary Meaning," *Trademark Reporter* 60, No. 3, May–June 1970, 263.

[2] McCarthy, J. Thomas. *Trademarks and Unfair Competition* (Rochester, N.Y.: The Lawyers Co-Operative Publishing Co., 1973), pp. 513–66.

[3] Ibid., p. 363.

[4] Diamond, Sidney A. *Trademark Problems and How to Avoid Them* (Chicago: Crain Communications, Inc., 1973), p. 51.

[5] *Thomas Register of American Manufacturers* (New York: Thomas Publishing Co., published annually).

[6] Diamond, p. 40.

[7] *Thomas Register.*

Chapter 5

[1]*The Trademark Register of the United States* (Washington, D.C.: The Trademark Register, published annually).

[2]*Thomas Register of American Manufacturers* (New York: Thomas Publishing Co., published annually).

[3]Campbell, Francis W., and Cohen, Jerry. *Trademark Selection and Protection,* Corporate Practice Series #18 (Washington, D.C.: The Bureau of National Affairs, 1979).

[4]Diamond, Sidney A. *Trademark Problems and How to Avoid Them* (Chicago: Crain Communications, Inc., 1973).

[5]*Trademark Selection—The Management Team Method* (New York: The United States Trademark Association, 1960).

Chapter 6

[1]U.S. Department of Commerce Patent and Trademark Office, *Trademark Rules of Practice of the Patent and Trademark Office with Forms and Statutes,* ninth ed., December 1976, revised May 1979.

[2]Schwartz, Albert. "Minimum Use Requirements for Foreign Trademark Owners," *Trademark Reporter* 69, No. 2, March–April 1978, 148.

[3]Kegan, Esther O. "Trademark 'Use'—Fact or Fiction?" *Trademark Reporter* 55, No. 3, March 1965, 175.

[4]*Trademark Rules of Practice,* sections 2.161 and 2.162.

[5]*International Classification of Goods and Services to Which Trade Marks Are Applied,* published jointly by The Patent Office of the United Kingdom of Great Britain and Northern Ireland, London, and United International Bureaux for the Protection of Intellectual Property, Geneva.

[6]*Trademark Rules of Practice,* sections 2.87 and 2.88.

[7]Ibid., sections 2.101 and 2.102.

[8]Ibid., p. 126.

Chapter 7

[1]Diamond, Sidney A. *Trademark Problems and How to Avoid Them* (Chicago: Crain Communications, Inc., 1973), p. 223.

[2] Borchard, William M. "When ® Should and Should Not Be Used," *Executive Newsletter* No. 18, The United States Trademark Association, 1975.

[3] Ibid.

Chapter 9

[1] McCarthy, J. Thomas. *Trademarks and Unfair Competition* (Rochester, N.Y.: Lawyers Co-Operative Publishing Co., 1973), p. 423.

[2] The United States Trademark Association, *Executive Newsletter* No. 23, 1977.

Chapter 10

[1] Gilson, Jerome. *Trademark Protection and Practice* (New York: Matthew Bender, Publisher, 1974 with subsequent supplements), p. 9.7.

[2] United States Patent and Trademark Office, "Trademark Registration Treaty," *Official Gazette* No. 973, August 1, 1978, p. 3.

Chapter 11

[1] McQuade, Walter. "Packagers Bear Up Under a Bundle of Regulations," *Fortune*, May 7, 1979, p. 180. Although an article on packaging, several excellent design firms are mentioned and examples of their work are illustrated.

[2] Rosen, Ben. *The Corporate Search for Visual Identity* (New York: Van Nostrand Reinhold Company, 1970).

[3] Carter, David E. *Corporate Identity Manuals* (Ashland, Ky.: Century Communications Unlimited, Inc., 1976).

[4] Capitman, Barbara Baer. *American Trademark Designs* (New York: Dover Publications, Inc., 1976).

[5] Kuwayama, Yasaburo. *Trademarks and Symbols*, 2 vols. (New York: Van Nostrand Reinhold Company, 1973).

Bibliography

"An Assault on the Trademark." *Business Week*, 10 April 1978, p. 80L.

Backman, Jules. "The Role of Trademarks in Our Competitive Economy." *Trademark Reporter* 58, no. 4: p. 219.

Barach, Arnold B. *Famous American Trademarks*. Washington, D.C.: Public Affairs Press, 1971.

Barnaby, Howard B., Jr. "Selection and Use of Trademarks—A Lawyer's Viewpoint." *The United States Trademark Association Executive Newsletter* no. 20 (1976). (Hereafter *USTA Executive Bulletin*.)

Bevan, Malcolm G. "Memorandum on the Creation of the EEC Trade Mark." *European Law Review*, April 1971, p. 134.

Brooks, John. "The Marts of Trade—It Will Grow on You." *The New Yorker*, 10 March 1973, p. 106. An account of the name change from Standard Oil Company (New Jersey) to Exxon Corporation.

Calimafde, John M. *Trademarks and Unfair Competition*. Brooklyn, N.Y.: Central Book Co., 1970.

Campbell, Hannah. *Why Did They Name It——?* New York: Fleet Publishing Company, 1964.

Carlton, Leonard. "The Oldtime Name Game." *Advertising Age*, 29 November 1971, p. 37.

"Cartier Plans to Open Store Near Mexico Rival." *The New York Times*, 19 June 1980, p. D-5.

Cooper, George W. "A Strategy for Registering Trademarks Abroad: A Middle-Sized Corporation Approach." *Trademark Reporter* 60, no. 3 (May–June 1970), p. 301.

"A Crackdown on Fake Brand-Name Products." *Business Week*, 23 October 1978, p. 53.

Davi, T. Richard. "Establishing a Strong Corporate Identity." *Industrial Management*, December 1977, p. 44.

Derenberg, Walter J. "The Walter J. Derenberg Memorial Edition." *The Trademark Reporter* 68, no. 3 (May–June 1978).

Detman, Art, Jr. "Trademarks in Danger." *USTA Executive Newsletter*, no. 13, August 1973. (Reprinted from *Sales Management—The Marketing Magazine*, 1973.)

Diamond, Sidney A. "Ladybug Case Illustrates Basic Trademark Principles." *Trademark Reporter* 60, no. 3 (May–June 1970), p. 353.

Diamond, Sidney A. "The Historical Development of Trademarks." *Trademark Reporter* 65, no. 4 (July–August 1975), p. 265.

Enis, Ben M. "Exxon Marks the Spot." *Journal of Advertising Research* 18, no. 6 (December 1978), p. 7.

Ettore, Barbara. "Sporting Emblems Sell Shirts." *The New York Times*, 13 June 1980, p. D-1.

Fey, Dorothy. "What's in a Name?" *The Practical Lawyer* 24, no. 8 (December 1978), p. 75.

Gordon, Neal. "What's in a name?" *USTA Executive Newsletter* no. 24, 1977.

Graham, Ellen. "The Image Makers." *The Wall Street Journal*, March 1, 1978.

"The Growing Tug-of-War Over Trademarks." *Business Week*, 4 November 1972, p. 64.

Hanak, Elmer William III. "The Quality Assurance Function of Trademarks." *Trademark Reporter* 65, no. 4 (July–August 1975), p. 318.

Holcomb, Charles A. *Trademarks—An Orientation for Advertising People.* New York: American Association of Advertising Agencies, 1971.

Howard, Niles. "Trademarks Under Fire." *Dun's Review*, September 1978, p. 104.

Joyce, Joseph J. "How to Select and Protect a Trademark." *Product Marketing*, May 1977.

Klooster, John W. *The Granting of Inventive Rights.* Minneapolis: Intel-Lux Inc. Publications, 1965.

Lunsford, Julius R., Jr. "Trademark Basics." *Trademark Reporter* 59, no. 12 (December 1969), p. 873.

Lunsford, Julius R., Jr. "Trademark Dilution and Deception." *Trademark Reporter* 63, no. 1 (January–February 1973), p. 41.

Lunsford, Julius R., Jr. "Trademark: A Priceless Asset." *Commerce Magazine*, April 1973.

Mahoney, Tom. "Protecting Your Corporate Trademarks." *USTA Executive Newsletter* no. 14 (November 1973).

Marquis, Harold H. *The Changing Corporate Image*. American Management Association, Inc., New York, 1974.

Merchant, J. H. "Deceptive and Descriptive Marks." *Trademark Reporter* 56, no. 3 (March 1966), p. 141.

Parcels, Roy. "A Closer Look at International Trademarks." *USTA Executive Newsletter* no. 19, 1975.

"The Question of Trademarks." *Modern Packaging* 35, no. 1 (September 1961).

Roberts, Tod A. "The Status Trademark." *USTA Executive Newsletter* no. 27, 1978.

Ruzan, Irving. "Trademarks and Trademark Searches." *Case & Comment*, September–October 1975.

Safire, William. "What's in a Name?" *The New York Times Magazine*, 5 August 1979, p. 7.

Schiro, Anne-Marie. "In Pursuit of Jewelry Lookalikes." *The New York Times*, 11 March 1980, p. B-15.

Solomon, Stephen. "Formica's Fight for Its Own Name." *Fortune*, 10 September 1979, p. 134.

Stessin, Lawrence. "Corporate Shootout Over Brand Names." *USTA Executive Newsletter* no. 26, 1978.

"They Say There's No Substitute for a Brandname." *Chemical Week*, 15 August 1979, p. 45.

United States Department of Commerce, Patent and Trademark Office. *Q & A About Trademarks*. 1977.

United States Department of Commerce, Patent and Trademark Office. *General Information Concerning Trademarks*. 1979.

The United States Trademark Association. *The Secretary's Guide to the Love and Care of Trademarks*. 1970.

The United States Trademark Association. *One Hundred Years of*

Service. 1978. (Anniversary brochure describing foundation, aims, and development of the USTA.)

White, Wm. Wallace, and Ravenscroft, Byfleet B. *Trademarks Throughout the World.* 3d ed. New York: Trade Activities, Inc., 1979. Edited by Anna Marie Greene. (Digest of laws of various countries, classification systems. Detailed description of classes of the International System. Trademark conventions.)

"Your Trademark: Registering Isn't Enough." *Marketing Image,* May–June 1971, p. 28.

Index

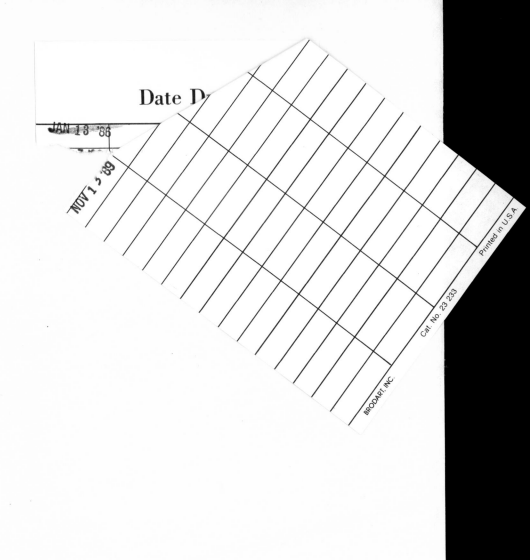

Date Due

BRODART, INC.

Cat. No. 23 233

Printed in U.S.A.

AMOCO

FOXBORO

SWF Machinery

A SUBSIDIARY OF SOUTHWEST FOREST INDUSTRIES

POLYTOP ®

TV GUIDE

TRIANGLE PUBLICATIONS INC.

Dan River

ℜROOTS

CLYSAR ®

SHRINK FILM

DU PONT

REG US PAT & TM OFF

HUNT·WESSON FOODS

Gilbarco

Templar Food Products